Exploring Asheville

∞∞

Its History, Attractions, Mysteries, Ghosts, and Tall Tales

The stories herein are neither indisputable fact nor total fiction. The informational stories are no more accurate than the public information relied on by the author. Some of the stories are rather obviously fictitious, or at least questionable, and should not be considered real or factual. While some of the names, characters, places, and incidents are real, others contained in the stories are products of the author's imagination.

Library of Congress Control Number: 2021923102

Published by I-65 North, Inc.
Nashville, Tennessee

Visit
www.tomcollinsauthor.com

Cover Design by Tom Trebing

Also by M. Thomas (Tom) Collins

MARK ROLLINS ADVENTURE SERIES:

Mark Rollins' New Career & the Women's Health Club
Mark Rollins and the Rainmaker
Mark Rollins and the Puppeteer
The Claret Murders, a Mark Rollins Adventure
Diversion, a Mark Rollins Adventure
Beyond Visual Range, a Mark Rollins Adventure

PROFESSIONAL GUIDANCE AND TRAVEL GENRE:

The Language of Excellence
Stories from Applewood Manor

Exploring Asheville

∞∞

Its History, Attractions, Mysteries, Ghosts, and Tall Tales

by

TOM COLLINS

Acknowledgement

Much of this book's content was adapted from my series titled Stories from Applewood Manor *that appeared originally on the internet website of the historic Asheville bed and breakfast inn, Applewood Manor (Circa 1912) located at 62 Cumberland Circle, Asheville, NC 28801. The inn's Rocking Chair Porch also serves as the venue for the telling of Tall Tales in part four of the book.*

My thanks to the city of Asheville, North Carolina, for making storytelling about the city and its neighboring areas easy. Few other places are as rich in history and human creativity, providing an inexhaustible supply of stories to tell. As usual, I thank my wife for her help in getting all the letters in the right order and for standing up for the reader.

Asheville has been called many things: Weirdest, Happiest, Quirkiest, Most Haunted Place in America, Santa Fe of the East, New Age Capital of the World, Paris of the South, Sky City, Beer City USA, and Land of the Sky. It has many secrets, mysteries, and legends—some factual, some alleged, some exaggerated and some hard to believe at all.

CONTENTS

EXPLORING ASHEVILLE
PART ONE

∞

Moments in the History of the City

Introduction

No HISTORY OF Asheville can be complete without telling the story of the mountains. They are the soul of Western North Carolina and its favorite city, Asheville.

As the continental plates moved closer together about 270 million years ago, the continents that were ancestral to North America and Africa collided creating majestic mountains once taller than those of the Rockies and within them stores of immense wealth in mineral resources. Huge masses of rock including those from the ocean floor were pushed westward along the margin of North America and piled up to form that we now know as the Appalachian Mountains. The building of the mountains continued for millions of years as blocks of con-tinental crust rode across one another, some rocks becoming so hot that they melted. There were volcanic eruptions and quiet lava flows, and as the molten rock cooled deep below ground, it crystallized to form granite. Some cooled slowly forming coarse-grained veins that became the source of minerals, such as quartz and mica, and gemstones, including emeralds.

Eventually, the building up of the mountain range ceased, and the continents began drifting apart. For the last 100 million years, erosion and weather has been carving away the mountains. Eroded rocks and soil spilled into streams and rivers becoming the building materials for North Carolina's coastal plain and its beaches and barrier islands. What remains is only the core of the original majestic mountain range; yet they remain the tallest mountains in the eastern U.S. What they lost in height they have gained in beauty and mystique that draws millions to them yearly from all over the world. The have become healing medicine for the soul and body, dispensing calming tranquility together with healing sun and high mountain air—perhaps aided by the power of their quartz laden soil.

While the mountains' rocks are billions of years old, people came only recently to the land. About twelve thousand years ago, ocean levels dropped due to the ice age. Native American ancestors walked on a newly exposed land bridge from present-day Siberia to Alaska. As their population grew, they spread into Canada, the Great Plains, and the Eastern Woodlands including the area we now call North Carolina. By 1600, more than a hundred thousand Native Americans made the mountains their home and the area became known as the Cherokee Nation. As the population of Europeans and their descendants expanded in North America, they migrated to the mountains to buy, settle, and farm the fertile bottomlands and hillsides in the region. The journey was difficult. They came by foot, wagon, or horseback, entering the area through gaps such as Swannanoa, Hickory Nut, Gillespie, and Deep Gaps. Others came south from Virginia, Maryland, and Pennsylvania. The completion of the Buncombe Turnpike in 1827 which followed the French Broad River opened the area to commerce and tourism. Farmers could now use their wagons to transport crops and livestock to market. As wagons, carriages, and stagecoaches replaced foot and horseback traffic, Asheville was on track to become a popular tourist destination.

The city was settled soon after the American Revolution at a crossroads of trails and on hunting grounds of Native American Indians along the French Broad River. The area benefited from the mountains' protection against weather extremes. That favorable climate may have contributed to the area being a place the American Indians sent their ill and wounded to heal. Its popularity grew rapidly--first from the discovery of gold in western North Carolina in the 1820s and 1830s. It was, however, the coming of the Western North Carolina Railroad in 1880 that really gave Asheville its biggest boost. The start of regular rail service ushered in a cycle of economic boom. The region's reputation as a haven for those seeking better health, became the main driving force behind Asheville's growth. That was only accelerated as "psychics" from around the world became interested in the power of the mountains' quartz and their belief that it had many energy and paranormal vortexes.

Modern times for Asheville really began in about 1888 when George Washington Vanderbilt, a twenty six year old member of the prominent and wealthy Vanderbilt family, commissioned architect, Richard Morris Hunt, and landscape architect, Frederick Law Olmsted, to create Biltmore House and Estate. Builders and artisans brought from Europe to build Biltmore stayed on in Asheville to work on other structures, and downtown Asheville. The result was a unique distinctive architectural character that continues to this day. Likewise, Asheville's unique qualities and the lure of its quartz laden mountains brought the mystics and gifted, the poor farmers and the gold rushers, the rich and famous, the talented and ar-tistic, the sick and the healers, the builders and dreamers—all to become its citizens. The next few pages tell the story of some of those people and moments in time that shape Asheville and forged its lasting character.

Asheville Cure

THE CURATIVE POWERS that have drawn people to Asheville are not a recent discovery. Native Americans had long brought their sick and injured to the area to recover. So, it is not surprising that when tuberculosis became the scourge of the American landscape that physicians would send their patients to these healing mountains. By 1900, the disease had killed one in seven of all people that had ever lived! Consumption or tuberculosis patients sought the "Asheville Cure" in sanatoriums where it was believed that rest and a healthful climate could change the course of the disease. Medical professionals at the turn of the century identified the city as having an optimum combination of barometric pressure, temperature, humidity, and sunlight believed to be conducive to healing tuberculosis.

With the arrival of the railroad in 1880, the Asheville Cure was suddenly only a day's travel away from cities on the East Coast and the hot humid cities of the South. The train opened the floodgates and tourists poured into the healing city to improve their health, prompting the development of hotels, boarding houses, bed and breakfast inns, and sanitaria.

Many of the country's rich and famous came to Asheville, some seriously ill. Many came just because of the area's reputation for improving one's general health and well-being. Some of those visitors stayed. And those that did contributed to its architecture, culture, and its sense of place. George Vanderbilt, who accompanied his ailing mother, fell in love with the area and built the fabulous Biltmore Estate, reclaiming eroded lands and advancing the science of agriculture and forestry. The Grove Park Inn was built by Edwin W. Grove who came to Asheville as a patient. By 1930, Asheville had 20 tuberculosis specialists and 25 sanitaria with a total of 900 beds.

The town is still a health center where people come for specialized treatment. Mission Hospital and the many specialists located nearby have made Asheville the prime medical center for Western North Carolina. The City's emphasis on the quality of life led many therapists, acupuncturists, and other alternative health care practitioners to set up shop in the city. Asheville was, and continues to be, a place to heal mind, body, and soul.

Battery Park Hotel

GIVEN THE DOMINANCE of this landmark over the heart of the city, you will never be considered Asheville smart until you know the history of the Battery Park Hotel and its role in the development of city. Of course, today's Battery Park Hotel looks nothing like the spectacular original Queen Anne version it replaced. That original was built in 1886 by Colonel Frank Coxe to accommodate tourists as Asheville gained recognition as a destination. The Coxe family was one of the oldest and most affluent in the state, and Colonel Coxe was also Vice President of Western North Carolina Railroad. Battery Park soon attracted the rich and famous from across all the United States and Europe. For almost a half century, it was Asheville's most prominent landmark towering over the city from its lofty perch on the eighty-foot-high Battery Porter Hill that was formerly the site of a Civil War battery. The hotel was a magnificent edifice, three stories high. Each room had its own fireplace, and verandahs provided guests with extraordinary mountain views. It was the height of elegance for the times and quite advanced technologically, with electric lights and elevators.

When Coxe died, the medicine magnate, Edwin Wiley Grove, who had adopted the city after a visit, purchased the hotel. Although he initially planned to continue its operation, it became clear that after fifty years the old hotel's day had passed. Automobile tourists were outnumbering train travelers, and it had become too expensive to keep up. Besides,

Grove had come up with a brilliant visionary idea. He razed the building, leveled the hill, and flattened the site. He built the Grove Arcade and his new modern hotel, giving his new hotel the same name as its predecessor. The Arcade breathed badly needed new life into Asheville's city center. Unfortunately, WWII put the business district back to sleep in 1942, when the Arcade was commandeered by the military for war purposes. Twenty years later the buildings were returned to the city, and the Arcade has been reborn to fulfill Grove's vision of a vibrant hub for commercial activity, tourist shopping and dining and night life in the city.

Built in 1924, the new fourteen story Battery Park Hotel was designed by W. L. Stoddard of New York and constructed with reinforced concrete, faced with brick, limestone, and terra cotta trim with a Mission Revival style roof. Its 220-rooms featured the very latest in convenience and terraces provided breathtaking views of the city and surrounding mountain vistas. The design was characteristic of 1920s hotel architecture—a mix of Neoclassical and "Spanish romanticism". It was according to Asheville's famous author, Thomas Wolfe, "as being stamped out of the same mold, as if by some gigantic biscuit-cutter of hotels that had produced a thousand others like it all over the country." The hotel has had its share of notoriety and is reputed to have its own ghost—perhaps more than one. Helen Clevenger, a 19-year-old college student, was found dead in Room 224 on July 17, 1936, having died the night before. She had been shot in the chest and slashed in the face with a sharp instrument. A hall boy at the hotel, 22-year-old Martin Moore, confessed to the murder, and was executed on December 11 of the same year. Over the years following her murder, hotel staff and guests have told haunting stories of seeing her spirit in the halls and of unusual unexplained paranormal events in

Room 224. Then in 1943, a U. S. Government Official, Clifton Alheit, jumped to his death off the roof of the Battery Park Hotel in an apparent suicide only to be followed by a similar event in 1972. To this day, people have been known to report seeing ghostly images of something or someone falling from the roof of the building. Today the building is still standing guard over the Grove Arcade; however, it ceased to operate as a hotel on October 30, 1972. Today it is owned by National Church Residences primarily as a residence for senior citizens. There are commercial businesses on the ground floor, but all the upper floors are now apartments for senior citizens.

Biltmore in WWII

THOSE WHO DO not learn from history are doomed to repeat it. In the War of 1812, British troops marched into Washington, D.C. on August 24, 1814 and torched the city, setting fire to the U.S. Capitol, the President's Mansion, and other landmarks. The events of 1814 were a reminder of what can happen in times of war.

By 1939, WWII was setting the world on fire. Events in Europe and the Far East were clear evidence of what could happen here should the war reach us. London was being shelled. Buckingham Palace had been damaged. Nazis were looting artwork from German-occupied countries. The Japanese were rampaging in the Far East and the Pacific. If the enemy could reach our lands, they would surely target our Capitol and other important national sites just as the 1814 enemy had.

David Finley, the director of the National Gallery of Art in Washington, D.C., was one of those raising the alarm over the risks to our national treasure of irreplaceable art and documents. Some of our most valuable items were concentrated in Washington. The risk of the status quo was too big. Finley was not one to sit idly by and wait for others to act. What was needed was a place far outside of D.C. where valuable items could be stored for safekeeping. He found an answer, the perfect place through his longtime friendship with Edith Vanderbilt. The Vanderbilt's Biltmore Estate was built of brick and steel with a limestone veneer. It was practically fireproof!

And its remote mountain location provided a natural shelter against the ravages of war.

Three weeks after the bombing of Pearl Harbor, 62 paintings (including the George Washington portrait by Gilbert Stuart) and 17 sculptures from the National Gallery of Art were crated and loaded onto a train for the trip through the foothills and mountains to the Biltmore Estate. Millions of dollars' worth of art, including pieces by Vermeer, Van Dyck, Goya, and Rembrandt, arrived in Asheville in the middle of a snowstorm. The paintings were stored in an unfinished room on the ground floor at Biltmore. The estate retrofitted the room, installing steel vaulted doors and vertical steel shelving from which the paintings could be hung. They also added draperies over those steel vaulted doors so nothing would look out of place. The art remained at Biltmore until 1944, when the wartime threat had begun to wane. The National Gallery issued press releases and invited photographers to shoot the art being loaded onto moving vans for the return journey to Washington. But until then, the war-time plan to save our treasures remained a closely held secret.

We may never know the full extent of the WWII relocation of our art and precious documents. The Biltmore story focused on the National Gallery of Art, but what about the Library of Congress and government agencies? There are rumors that subterranean Asheville may have also played a safekeeping role and that some artifacts may yet remain in caverns lost or forgotten.

Cold Mountain

THE BESTSELLING NOVEL, *Cold Mountain* (1997), was written by the author Charles Frazier, a native of Asheville. Coming from the city that boasts names like Wolfe, Fitzgerald, and O. Henry, Frazier joins a host of contemporary Asheville authors carrying forward the city's rich literary history— authors such as Sarah Addison Allen, Sara Gruen, Gail Godwin, John Ehle, Wiley Cash, Denise Kiernan, Wilma Dykeman, and the list goes on.

The question is why Asheville has given rise to so many successful authors and Frazier had an answer in a 2017 interview. It is "Asheville itself…the literary history of this small city is amazing." He explains the strong oral history tradition of the mountain people. "That old Celtic kind of thing is certainly a big part of it. The Cherokee oral tradition is still alive. A lot of us here grew up hearing stories—hearing hunting tales and ghost stories—told by older folks…When I go to family reunions, there's a sharing of the history, the stories about those in our family, walking through the cemeteries and learning about our ancestors."

Asheville is the place where this bestselling author found the inspiration for his craft in the area's local history and unique culture. It is in the mountains where his novels take their voice:

Whenever I'm back in those mountains, I feel like that's home, no matter how long I've been away. That's the place

*I know the best, and the place that in my imagination
sums up all those things about being rooted and knowing
a place and having a place.*

The Frazier family has lived in the mountains around
Asheville for over 200 years and he draws on that history
in telling his *Cold Mountain* story based on the experiences
of a real life great-grand-uncle. In the novel W. P. Inman,
a wounded deserter from the Confederate army, walks for
months to return to his mountain home and Ada Monroe, the
love of his life.

Few people realize that Cold Mountain is a real place—
a high spot within the Pisgah National Forest just 35 scenic
miles southwest of the "Land of Sky" as Asheville was once
called. There is not an actual town of Cold Mountain, however. The mountain itself (elevation 6,030 feet) is part of the
Shining Rock Wilderness area in Pisgah National Forest. It is
still in its natural state much as it was during the Civil War.
You can enjoy beautiful views of the mountain from the Blue
Ridge Parkway, but to reach the summit requires a strenuous
10-mile roundtrip hike.

Edwin Wiley Grove and his Pig Baby

TRY TO VISUALIZE an advertisement with the image of a pig that has the face of a baby and the words, "Makes Children and Adults as Fat as Pigs" written across the body of the pig. Underneath that image is the name of the product being promoted, "Grove's Tasteless Chill Tonic."

While today the ad featuring a pig with a baby's head might not cause you to part with your fifty cents, by 1890 it was selling more bottles of Grove's Tasteless Chill Tonic than Coca-Cola. If it had not been for the pig baby, there probably would not be a Grove Park or Grove Park Inn.

Malaria was a wide-spread problem in the United States throughout the 19th century and well into the twentieth century. George Washington and even Abraham Lincoln were reported to suffer from bouts of malaria. Malaria, especially in the Southern states, like tuberculosis, was a killer. More people may have died from malaria than any other cause. Until the 1930s, quinine with its unpleasant bitter taste, was the only effective malaria treatment.

Edwin Wiley Grove was convinced that whoever could produce a tasteless quinine tonic would make a fortune. And in 1878 working in Paris, Tennessee, he invented his Grove's Tasteless Chill Tonic. Grove had mixed, or suspended, quinine in a sweet syrup with lemon flavoring. The truth is, it was not tasteless and was unlikely to have fattened children or adults. Consider this comment posted on the National Museum of American History's web site:

As a child ...my siblings and l were given chill tonic for everything from a cut or cold or punishment. It was the most disgusting thing l have ever tasted. I think the maker of this tonic should be drawn and quartered...or given the tonic for life.

Nevertheless, the quinine was genuinely an effective ingredient in combating malaria and the ad worked—so it flew off the shelves. And the Pig Baby was on the way to making Grove's fortune.

With his doctor's urgings, in 1897 Grove with his family began spending their summers in Asheville to benefit from its healthy clean mountain air. Like others who did so, he fell in love with the city and through his investments, including the Grove Park Inn, he helped shape Asheville into the alluring destination it is today.

F. Scott Fitzgerald

MOST OF US have read *The Great Gatsby* by the American author, F. Scott Fitzgerald (1896-1940), or one of his other novels such as *This Side of Paradise, Tender is the Night* or *The Curious Case of Benjamin Button.* But did you know that he has a tumultuous connection to Asheville?

Fitzgerald spent two summers in the city that draws the rich and famous to its clear mountain air for rest, relaxation and repair of body and soul. It was 1935 and 1936. Fitzgerald rented two rooms at the famous Grove Park Inn, one for sleeping and the other for writing. They say he rented those particular rooms so he could see the main entrance to watch the cars pulling up and observe interesting people and how they were dressed—probably for material for stories that never got written—characters that he could portray in the age he belonged to when gin was the national drink and sex was an obsession. It was about jazz and flappers.

Unfortunately, his Asheville stay was neither a productive nor a happy one. His glamorous life of parties and jazz clubs was falling apart as was his marriage. His wife, the once beautiful, brilliant Zelda Fitzgerald, diagnosed as schizophrenic, was wrestling with her demons just across the valley from the Grove Park Inn at Asheville's Highland Hospital. While it is a different story, one I will tell in another piece, she would die there in a tragedy of the type that gives rise to the haunted reputation of the historic Montford district of Asheville.

Brian Railsback, who was dean of the Honors College at Western Carolina University, says, "Fitzgerald was at a low point. He was drinking 50 ponies of beer a day — the "beer cure" — in an attempt to wean himself off gin. His writing, 10 years after *The Great Gatsby*, had gone flat. He was churning out hack stories for magazines, trying to pay off debts and the bills... This was a place where he hoped that he would be restored, find discipline and then maybe find subject matter."

While Railsback's explanation for the reasons Fitzgerald came to Asheville may be correct, there was another one. He was suffering from tuberculosis, and Asheville is where one went for relief. Nevertheless, it appears that Fitzgerald, who turned forty while at the Grove Park Inn, spent much of his time in an alcoholic haze. That may explain the bad dive into the Inn's swimming pool that left him with a broken shoulder, or the separate incident where he fell in the bathroom and was found on the floor the next morning, and yet another time when he fired a pistol in one of the two rooms he rented.

F. Scott Fitzgerald packed his bags and left Asheville in 1937 for Hollywood to accept a writing job for the movies. It was there, with the encouragement of a woman lover, that he began drinking less and writing seriously. He started work on *The Last Tycoon*. He died there in 1940 after a heart attack leaving *The Last Tycoon* to be finished and published posthumously by his friend Edmund Wilson, a critic and writer. His wife, Zelda, outlived her husband by eight years, much of them spent in Asheville's Highland Hospital where she, along with the other patients, died in a tragic fire that destroyed the hospital. The two, husband and wife, were rejoined together in a small Catholic cemetery in suburban Maryland.

George W. Pack

THE WINTER OF 1895 was quite unusual across the United States. Florida's deep freeze wiped out most of the citrus groves. The weather alternated between unusually warm periods with intermittent extreme winter storms and deep snowfalls. The Asheville winter was particularly harsh. What occurred on February 16th of that year was extraordinary. George Willis Pack, a Cleveland Ohio based lumber tycoon with a fondness for Asheville, sent a dispatch to Asheville's mayor that included the following instructions:

> Do your citizens need help on account of the severe weather? If so, draw on me for such amount as you think proper.

According to John Turk, an Asheville tour guide, and Professor Emeritus, at Youngstown State University, for anyone who knew Pack, this act of generosity would have come as no surprise.

In 1884, George Pack's wife traveled to Asheville hoping that its helpful climate would ease her respiratory difficulties. She experienced a marked improvement in her health. Like many others who visited Asheville, her husband developed a strong attraction to what he considered a mountain paradise—one ripe for growth. However, initially boarding at one of the city's finer establishments, the Swannanoa Hotel, what they experienced was not quite up to their personal standards—which included a lack of indoor plumbing. So, Pack had a residence built on Merrimon Avenue for use during return trips to the city. It was not your typical vacation home. "Manyoaks" was one of Asheville's largest estates. Then he began purchasing land and property, investing heavily in the development of the downtown and surrounding areas of his adopted city, often referring to himself as an Ashevillian.

Pack established a free kindergarten for Asheville, donating the cost of the land and building as well as funding the teacher's salary. He donated prime real estate for a new Asheville court-house and to expand the city's central square. He donated the building for the Public Library.For more than twenty years, he continued to contribute to the betterment of Asheville, providing financial aid for city hospitals, the YMCA, orphans and widows, and veterans' organizations. He also deeded land for three city parks. His gifts were often provided by means of a brief note to city officials. His gifts *"were always timely and of an enduring value."* The Asheville Citizen newspaper in 1901 wrote:

> *We salute George W. Pack! If heaven has vouchsafed to any community a better citizen, the fame of him has not reached these parts.*

Despite his fondness for Asheville, Pack continued to maintain his permanent residence in Cleveland. And around 1900, he and his wife moved to a shore-side residence located on Southampton Long Island at the advice of doctors who recommended a move to sea level due to Pack's failing heart. After the move he never returned to the mountain city he had adopted, and on August 31, 1906, Asheville's greatest philan-thropist died.

Isaac Dickson

ANOTHER EARLY CITIZEN of Asheville to make an enduring mark on the city was Isaac Dickson--the first person of color appointed to the Asheville City School Board. In 1892, he convinced Dr. Edward Stephens, principal of Asheville's first public school for African American Students, that Ashville needed a YMCA-like facility for black men. Dickson and Stephens approached George Vanderbilt, founder of the Biltmore Estate, with the idea for their "Young Men's Institute."

They couched their proposal in terms of helping the black construction workers employed at the Biltmore Estate: "to improve the moral fiber of the black male through education focusing on social, cultural, business and religious life." Moved by their presentation, Vanderbilt loaned the organization $32,000 for a building to be designed by one of the Biltmore Estate architects, Richard Sharp Smith.

The Young Men's Institute Building, also known as the YMI Building, opened in 1893. Today the two ½ story, 18,000 square foot building of pebbledash coated masonry with accents of brick, stone and wood is on the National Register of Historic Places. The facility was the true center of the civic, cultural, and business life of Asheville's black community. It featured a public library and classes for children and adults, dormitory, and athletic facilities. It served as a social and spiritual center and included office space on the ground floor for a doctor, pharmacist, barber, undertaker, and restaurant. By 1910 it had its own orchestra.

As times changed the need for a separate facility for black men faded. In 1980, a coalition of nine black churches, with the support of both the black and white communities, bought the YMI. The new owners restored the building and re-established it as a Cultural Center. Today, organized around five core components (community programming, community forums, cultural exhibitions, economic literacy and fifth, an annual cultural festival), it continues to serve the black community. The building is now more commonly known as the YMI Cultural Center.

The annual three day cultural festival, known as Goombay, is a display of sights, sounds, and tastes of the African-Caribbean. The free event delivers a variety of entertainment including dancing and the beating of West African drums ringing with the harmonic live music featuring gospel, reggae, funk, and soul.

After more than a hundred and twenty five years, Isaac Dickson imprint on the city remains and his YMI Building is still used to promote and celebrate the black community of Asheville.

Lady on the Hill—George Vanderbilt's Biltmore

I PURPOSELY HAVE not written much about the Biltmore Estate because it is perhaps, the most dominate aspect of Asheville, and there is no way that I can compete with the barrage of Biltmore history, facts, and publications you will encounter at every turn while in Asheville. It is for many what Asheville is known for, and it is what brings most people to Asheville. It is only after they arrive that they discover all the other riches of the city and its people. As a visitor here, you will probably learn more about the Biltmore than you had ever thought to ask. However, the Biltmore is so much a part of Asheville that I cannot ignore it. So, let me give you a few trivia facts:

- George Washington Vanderbilt visited Asheville in 1888 accompanying his ill mother who was seeking the healing benefits the city had become famous for. The young man of 26 was captivated by the area's natural beauty. A member of the wealthy Vanderbilt family, he slowly began purchasing land and ended up with 125,000 acres. The land was largely defoliated, abused farmland and farmers were apparently happy to take the young Vanderbilt's money.

- The Biltmore is George Vanderbilt's vision of a French Renaissance chateau with architectural features of 16th-century castles he had seen in the Loire Valley of France.

He was quite a traveler having made the voyage across the Atlantic to Europe 60 times during his life.

- Construction began in 1889. Vanderbilt brought talented craftsmen from Europe for the construction, and many stayed as the future builders of Asheville's commercial and government buildings as well as the residences of its citizens—thus giving the city its distinctive and unique architectural character.

- It took 1000 men six years to complete the Biltmore.

- To expedite the shipments of building materials, a railroad track was built from the main railway to the construction site.

- The architect of the estate's gardens, Frederick Law Olmsted, also created Central Park in New York City. The restoration of the land using sustaining management techniques brought forth an entirely new era of forest management in the U.S.

- The Biltmore is America's largest home with 250 rooms, 35 bedrooms, 43 bathrooms and 65 fireplaces.

- From 1941 to 1944, during World War II, the Biltmore house was used to secretly store the nation's treasure of irreplaceable art and documents.

- The estate was designated a National Historic Landmark in 1963, and it remains a major tourist attraction in Western North Carolina with 1.4 million visitors each year.

- Biltmore is among the country's most elaborately decorated homes during the Christmas holidays.

- Over 6,000 weddings occur at the Biltmore Estate each year.

- Biltmore is home to the most-visited U.S. winery. It spans 94 acres, sells 170,000 cases of wine, and sees 650,000 visitors annually.

- The grounds and buildings of Biltmore Estate have appeared in several major motion pictures and TV series including *Being There, The Last of the Mohicans, Forrest Gump, Patch Adams, Hannibal, One Tree Hill, The Private Eyes, The Swan, Tap Roots, The Pruitts of Southampton, A Breed Apart, Mr. Destiny,* and others.

The history of the Biltmore is told by Howard E. Covington in his book, *Lady on the Hill: How Biltmore Estate Became an American Icon,* available from Amazon.com and other retail sources.

Rafael Guastavino Moreno

ASHEVILLE'S MASTER BUILDER, Rafael Guastavino Moreno (1842-1908), was born in Valencia, Spain and immigrated to the United States in 1881 settling initially in New York City. He left Spain already acclaimed for his signature elements: grand arches, domes, and vaults crafted with interlocking stone or terra cotta tiles. Guastavino had developed a special method of building by reviving and improving on ancient forms of masonry construction. His methods became known as Guastavino Construction. Skilled artisans used layers of flat clay tiles embedded in mortar to build horizontal parts of buildings in the form of vaults or domes to carry floors, roofs, ceilings, and staircases. Aside from their desired artistic qualities, his structures were strong, lightweight, fireproof, and economical eliminating the need for steel and wood.

Soon the Guastavino Construction Method was being deployed in the homes of the rich and famous as well as important public and business buildings, including the National Museum of Natural History in Washington, D.C., New York City's Grand Central Station, the Boston Public Library, Carnegie Hall, and hundreds of other landmarks. In 1894, his reputation brought him to North Carolina to work on the Biltmore house. He fell in love with the area and began to buy land south of Black Mountain eventually accumulating about a thousand acres. He built a large house, the Rhododendron Estate, planted grape vines and apple trees, created ponds, and built workshops and kilns where he experimented with making the tiles he needed for his construction.

It is also in Asheville that Guastavino designed and built what he considered his greatest work, St. Lawrence Catholic Church (now a Basilica). What stands out singularly for this Guastavino site is its dome. It has a span of 58 by 82 feet and is reputed to be the largest, freestanding, elliptical dome in North America. And the mighty vault was built over nothing! The entire dome is made of thin, flat terra cotta tiles, 6 x 12 inches, and an inch thick. The tiles were laid as if shingling an imaginary dome in space, using only cement. Author Peter Austin described the process: "Beginning at the bottom course, the first six or seven thicknesses of tile were laid one over the other braking joints, in a special cement of plaster of paris. The next course, laid in Portland cement, was held in place by overlapping the tile below. The process was repeated until the great dome was finished without the aid of girdlers [sic] or supporting scaffolds."

Rafael Guastavino died at age 65 in 1908 after an abrupt onset of lung congestion and kidney complications. A high requiem mass was held for him in the nearly completed building which was completed by his son. And according to his dying wish, the great builder was interred within the walls of his greatest masterpiece. His wife, Francesca, was shattered by her husband's passing. At the time of his death, she is reported to have had the big clock in the tower of their Rhododendron Estate stopped to never run again. Ironically, Guastavino, known for fireproof structures, built his Rhododendron home, nicknamed the Spanish Castle, out of wood. A fire eventually destroyed it and Francesca was severely burned. She died in 1946 spending her final three years in an Asheville rest home.

O. Henry

IF YOU ARE short on pocket change, take a twenty-two minute walk, or one mile drive, from the center of town (the Grove Arcade) to 53 Birch Street, and you can pick up at least $1.87. Provided that is that you are not afraid of the dead! That is because your short walk, or one mile drive, will take you to the historic Riverside Cemetery. Inside the Cemetery, up a steep hill, is an unpretentious gravestone. The name carved on the stone is faded from years of exposure to the mountain air. The name is William Sydney Porter and the dates, barely readable, are 1862-1910.

Who was William Sydney Porter you ask? He was the famous author of about 400 short stories—probably America's greatest short story author! You know him by his pseudonym— O. Henry. And scattered across the stone and spilling over onto the grass is loose change—thrown there by visitors to the gravesite to make sure there is at least $1.87 remaining on the stone. That is the amount Della had left after paying her bills in O. Henry's famous story, *The Gift of the Magi*.

The fact that O. Henry is buried here is somewhat of a mystery since New York was his city. Although he was originally from Greensboro, North Carolina, New York is where he got his inspiration and did his writing. However, the train made travel between the two cities rather routine. Asheville was the home of his second wife, Sara Coleman. The two were estranged but often visited between the two cities. The famed short story author died June 5, 1910, in New York at age 48 because of cirrhosis of the liver, complications of diabetes and an enlarged heart. After the funeral services were held, his wife brought him to Asheville to be buried in Riverside Cemetery in the Montford community. His wife, Sara, lived until age ninety-one and is buried beside him.

The last story completed by O. Henry prior to his death, *Let Me Feel Your Pulse–Adventures in Neurasthenia* was written while he was in Asheville to restore his health. The story is somewhat autobiographical in that it is about a man from New York who consults many physicians and tries many medications to cure an unknown illness. In real life, O. Henry's time in Asheville did improve his health. Unfortunately, it was only a temporary change, because when he returned to New York he resumed his bad habits and death soon followed.

Station #4, on the Asheville Urban Trail pays tribute to O. Henry with the bronze image of a watch and comb, symbols from his well-known work, *The Gift of the Magi*. The bronze casting is located on Patton Avenue close to the Drhumor Building.

Thomas Wolfe

A VISITOR TO Asheville will quickly learn that American novelist, Thomas Wolfe (1900-1938), is the city's most beloved author. But it was not always so. Tom Wolfe was a genius with a photographic memory. He is said to have almost total recall. His thinly veiled descriptions of life and times in Asheville was so frank and realistic that his classic, *Look Homeward, Angel* (1929), was banned from Asheville's library for more than seven years. The town's anger and hatred over their portrayal was so strong that Wolfe stayed away for eight long years.

Thomas was born in Asheville in 1900, the last of eight children. He grew up in a boarding house, the Old Kentucky Home, owned by his mother, Julia Wolfe. She bought the boarding house at 48 Spruce Street in Asheville, taking up residence there with her young son, Tom. The rest of the family remained at the 92 Woodfin Street residence. His father, W. O. Wolfe ran a gravestone business as a successful stone carver. He used an angel in the window to attract customers. Thomas Wolfe "described the angel in great detail" in his novel *Look Homeward, Angel.* Thus, a replica welcomes visitors to his boarding house home, now called the Thomas Wolfe Memorial. At age fifteen or sixteen, Tom's father paid for him to attend the University of North Carolina and from there, he went on to study at Harvard.

His time in the boarding house was a period when tuberculosis was rampant in the country and Asheville was considered having the ideal climate for those suffering with the disease.

It is likely that some of the boarders at Old Kentucky Home were TB sufferers. And young Tom Wolfe may have been infected with the disease which apparently went into remission, although he writes to his mother in 1920 about a troubling cough and blood in his handkerchief.

Thomas Wolfe died at 37. It is said from his writings that he had a fear of TB, which haunted him and affected his writing long before the discovery of a tubercular lesion in his right lung following his death. It is believed that the lesion opened allowing TB cells to flow to his brain. He died of meningeal tuberculosis often called TB of the brain.

His grave is not far from O. Henry's plot in the Riverside Cemetery. The cemetery is in the Montford History District. If you visit his gravesite, you might take an extra pen to leave by his gravestone. It will join many other pens and pencils left by visitors in memory of this prolific great American novelist.

Thunder Road

ASHEVILLE HAS BEEN the site of several movies, but only one, *Thunder Road*, has had a lasting impact on American culture. The 1958 movie gave a whole new meaning to the words "thunder and lightning." It launched the muscle car era in America and introduced the world to mountain moonshine or "White Lightning"! Fast cars thundering through winding mountain roads running bootleg whisky served as the beginning from which NASCAR has grown into one of the premiere American sports.

The hot spot in Asheville in the fifties was the Sky Club, best described as a Supper Club—dinner, drinks, and dancing. At that time, liquor by the drink was illegal, but the Sky Club was not always strict in that regard. However, when Government Revenuers were onsite, they only sold ice and setups.

According to Asheville resident and historian, Jerry Sternberg, the most exciting event ever to take place at the Sky Club was when Robert Mitchum came to town to star in *Thunder Road*.

The whole town was star-struck, and one scene in the movie was shot in the restaurant. A couple of my friends took the entire week off from work just to be extras in the nightclub scene. Mitchum cut a wide swath [in Asheville]. He and his wife stayed at the Battery Park Hotel, and it was widely rumored that his mistress was staying down the street at the Vanderbilt. Mitchum spent most evenings at the Sky Club, though, drinking, dining, and dancing with the ladies who absolutely threw themselves at this tall, handsome movie star. I witnessed more than one violent confrontation precipitated by a husband's or boyfriend's jealous rage, but Mitchum was big enough to take care of himself—and, after all, all he was doing was dancing.

In *Thunder Road*, Robert Mitchum's character is a tough, resourceful veteran of the Korean War who returns home to carry on with the family business of making and running moonshine through the mountains. He must do battle with government agents intent on squelching the illicit trade, and at the same time, he has to deal with syndicate thugs out of Memphis looking to horn in on the business. The movie is reflective of the Scotch-Irish traditions for moonshining and fierce independence. Mitchum's character lives by the "don't tread on me" principle of personal freedom and self-reliance. He is portrayed as a peace-loving man with a long fuse, but he will only be pushed so far before pushing back. He insists on being his own man and living strictly by his own rules.

Exploring Asheville
Part Two

∞

Things to Do and See

Introduction

THE CITY OF Asheville is the jewel of Western North Carolina. Founded at the crossroads of Native American hunting trails along the French Broad River, the city is protected from weather extremes by the magnificent Blue Ridge Mountains. Over time it became an extraordinary place with a culturally diverse population—descendants of originally inhabiting Native Americans, as well as those of early immigrants, settlers, gold rushers. poor farmers, soldiers, slaves, free men, and free women. They were followed by the rich and famous, the talented and the artistic, the mystics and gifted, the sick and the healers, the builders, and the dreamers.

When I began writing about the city, I discovered that there is more to do and see in Asheville and its surrounding area than one can do in a lifetime. Its rich history and its copious human creativity provide an inexhaustible supply of stories to tell. The task of telling you all the things you can do and see in this extraordinary place is doomed to failure. Every time I thought I had written enough; I would make another discovery. Nevertheless, in this section, I will share with you those "things to do and see" that I have discovered so far. But, given Asheville's reservoir of creativity its citizens will add new things and new events in the future that will make the city even more wonderful.

Asheville Downtown

IF YOU ARE new to Asheville, the place to start exploring is its downtown area beginning with the Arcade Building. Locals call it the Grove Arcade. It is a beautiful historic mall that serves as the anchor of Asheville's city center. Downtown Asheville has its own unique feel and energy. It is a highly diverse place and host to a mix of culture, music, and art. It is where street performers abound among its museums, restaurants, and gorgeous stores. There are some one hundred restaurants and more than two hundred locally owned stores and boutiques. Dubbed the Paris of the South, among other names, Asheville can find almost any reason for a free street festival. You can walk to craft breweries, picnic in the park, or take any one of several guided tours including LaZoom Fun City Tour in a bright purple bus full of laughter, or the Rooftop Bar Tour for a scenic view of the city and its surrounding mountains. There is the self-guided tour of the Urban Trail. You can tour the Thomas Wolfe Memorial, the novelist's rambling and fascinating boyhood home located in the middle of town. At night, you might want to take a ghost tour or take in Asheville's night life. You will always find plenty of live music in center city.

There are five distinct shopping areas in Downtown Asheville:

1. The Grove Arcade—Its restaurants range from upscale ones to hot dogs and coffee shops. Outside dining is a favorite

activity for locals and tourists. And there are plenty of shops and galleries to visit.

2. Haywood Street—Whatever you are looking for you are likely to find on Haywood Street from furniture to chocolate with craft supplies, books, and art in between.

3. Wall Street—It is a pedestrian street with great restaurants and unique shops that is often called the most charming street in downtown Asheville.

4. Broadway & Biltmore—This area has lots of local color, like Mast General Store and Blue Sprial 1 Gallery along with restaurants and outdoor dining.

5. Lexington Avenue—The area is a unique collection of lo-cally owned boutiques, gift shops, restaurants, and galleries. Locals describe it as funky and eclectic. It has its own motto, "Where world culture meets counterculture."

The Grove Arcade is the city's center. Asheville is a walking town. If you are driving, you will want to park and explore the city on foot. For those comfortable on a bicycle, it is a great alternative way to get around without the hassle of finding parking places. There are several bike shops that rent bikes. Asheville Bicycle Co. is one—they will deliver and pickup, and they offer bikes for children as well as adults. Their phone number is (828) 774-5215. Electric bikes are another alterna-tive. The Flying Bike conducts electric bike tours exploring Asheville as well as renting bikes. Find out more by going to htps://flyingbiketours.com.

For another option, you can take is one of Asheville's trolley tours. I suggest the Gray Lines Hop-on/Hop Off Tour for flexibility. Learn more by going to https://graylineasheville.com/tours/hop-on-hop-off-tour/.

Arcade Building

THE PLACE TO shop and eat is the beautiful Grove Arcade in the center of downtown Asheville. Its official name is the Arcade Building, but you will find that everyone just calls it the Grove Arcade. What you might not know is the role it played during WWII. In 1942, largely because of the security of its remoteness, the building was commandeered by the United States Government for a wartime role. The existing merchants and other tenants were given a one month notice to vacate before the location was converted to the accounting office of the US Army. It would be sixty years before the Grove Arcade was restored and returned to its original civilian use as a center city mall for shops, restaurants, and business offices.

The idea for the Arcade came from E.W. Grove. He was a self-made millionaire who moved to Asheville in 1910 and began plans in 1920 to build the Arcade to enliven the downtown of the city he had come to love. He conceived of the Arcade as an elegant building that would be a new kind of retail center—in a sense he invented the mall. Architect Charles N. Parker designed the Arcade as a 5-story base with a 14-story tower, filled with shops, offices and living spaces. Grove died in 1927 prior to the completion of the Arcade. With his death, the 14-story tower was never built even though the five floor base was designed to support its addition. It opened in 1929 and quickly delivered on its promise, becoming the center of commercial and civic life in Western North Carolina. Tenants included candy and cigar stores, a haberdashery, a public

stenography office, fruit stands, millinery shops, beauty par-
lors and barbershops, a photography center, bookstalls, and
specialty groceries. Offices filled the upper floors. The Arcade
was closed in 1942 when the Federal Government took over the
building for war time purposes. Following the war, the Arcade
continued under Federal ownership and eventually became
the headquarters for the National Climatic Data Center. By
1997 the Government had discontinued use of the facility and
the City of Asheville acquired title to the building under the
National Monument Act. A restored Grove Arcade reopened
in 2002 after its sixty-year hiatus.

Today, the Arcade is considered one of North Carolina's
most historic and beautiful commercial buildings. Outside,
the Portico Market features farmers and craftspeople selling
their wares—including local crafts, honey, handmade soaps
and much more. Restaurants and shops occupy the first floor.
Most of the restaurants have outdoor sidewalk dining—a
prime evening spot in downtown Asheville for locals and tourists. The interior corridor features mostly shops and galleries.
Their offerings include fine local art, antiques, fine gifts, and
international cuisine. The second floor is reserved for business
offices, and the third through the fifth floors are residential
apartments referred to as The Residences at Grove Arcade.

While the sidewalk shops and restaurants are pet friendly,
pets are not allowed in the interior corridor where the most
serious shopping occurs. So, plan accordingly.

Asheville Urban Trail

ASHVILLE IS A walker's city. There is something new to see and enjoy with every step. And for art lovers there is the 1.7-mile Urban Trail through the streets of downtown Asheville. Public sculptures along the walk tell the story of Asheville's history. For Asheville natives each sculpture becomes a landmark for meetings or for giving directions. The trail was created as a continuing program to improve the quality of the Asheville cityscape through the display of public art. It was designed by volunteers and it was funded completely through donations from individuals, groups, and organizations. There are thirty stops along the trail, which begins at Pack Square. Each stopping point is a remembrance of a not-to -be-forgotten person, place, event, or time in the history of Asheville.

1. Walk into History: George Willis Pack

2. Crossroads: Turkeys & Pigs

3. Stepping Out: Bronze Top Hat

4. O. Henry: Plaque in sidewalk

5. Immortal Image: Drhumor Building

6. Elizabeth Blackwell, MD: Iron bench with a bower of medicinal herbs

7. Art Deco Masterpiece: S&W Building

8. Flat Iron Architecture: Giant flat iron

9. Catwalk: Cat on wall

10. Grove's Vision: Grove Arcade

11. Historic Hilltop: Battery Park Hotel

12. Guastavino's Monument: Basilica of St. Lawrence

13. Shopping Daze: Abstract, forged metal representation of three ladies shopping

14. Marketplace: Bronze bonnet and basket of apples on bench

15. Legacy of Design: Bench and young boy, Richard Sharp Smith

16. Woodfin House: Ceramic replica of YMCA

17. Wolfe's Neighborhood: Metal sculptures depicting items from Thomas Wolfe's life

18. Dixieland: Bronze replica of Thomas Wolfe's shoes in front of Thomas Wolfe Memorial

19. Curtain Calls: Abstract metal sculptures mounted on building

20. On the Move: Art in motion sculpture with the history of transportation - turn the wheel to hear 11 different sounds.

21. Civic Pride: Historic bell from City Hall

22. Past and Promise: Little girl drinks at a horse-head fountain

23. Man and Mountain: Plaque

24. Ellington's Dream: Granite etching of city-county buildings by Douglas Ellington.

25. Time Remembered: Plaque covers bicentennial time capsule

26. Monument Corner: Bronze carving tools and carving

27. Brick Artisan: James Vester Miller, cornucopia over the doorway

28. "The Block": Bronze wall sculpture for historic African American community

29. Hotel District: Bronze eagle overlooks early hotel district

Antique Car Museum

IF YOU ARE a car enthusiast, be sure to save some time to visit the Estes-Winn Antique Car Museum located in Grovewood Village adjacent to The Omni Grove Park Inn. For reference, it is only 2 ½ miles from the Grove Arcade at 111 Grovewood Rd. The museum was founded by Asheville's legend, Harry D. Blomberg, to showcase his prized collection of vintage automobiles, including a rare 1957 Cadillac Eldorado Brougham as well as antique automobiles dating back to the time of wooden steering wheels and polished brass headlights. Here are some of the cars on display:

- 1913 Ford Model T (Tin Lizzie)

- 1915 Ford Model T Touring Car (Copperhead)

- 1916 Willys Overland Touring

- 1925 Dodge Touring

- 1926 Cadillac Seven-Passenger Touring Sedan

- 1927 LaSalle Phaeton

- 1927 REO Flying Cloud

- 1928 Chandler Sedan

- 1928 Pontiac Sedan

- 1929 Chevrolet Sedan

- 1929 Ford Model A Coupe (with rumble seat)

- 1932 Chevrolet Coupe

- 1940 Buick Century

- 1940 Packard Coupe

- 1950 MG TD Roadster

- 1954 Cadillac Sedan

- 1957 Cadillac Eldorado Brougham

- 1959 Edsel Corsair

Harry D. Blomberg was one of Asheville's greatest bene-factors. He made a fortune in the automobile industry as Asheville's Cadillac-Pontiac dealer and remained an active businessman, civic leader, and leader in the Jewish community until his death in 1991. He belonged to the Kiwanis Club, the Masons, and the Shriners and served on the board of direc-tors of St. Joseph Hospital. He saved Julia Wolfe's boarding house, Old Kentucky Home, from demolition in 1941, then sold it back to the Wolfe family three months later because he believed it belonged to them. The house is now a memorial for Julia's son, famed author, Thomas Wolfe. Blomberg named the museum after Cathryn Estes, the first wife of General Motors president EM Estes, and Barbara Winn, granddaughter of Pontiac executive Lonnie Holmes.

There is more to meet the eye at Grovewood Village than automobiles. The historic site once housed the weaving and woodworking operations of Biltmore Industries, a force in American craft that was originally backed by Edith Vanderbilt. Listed on the National Register of Historic Places, the property serves as an arts and crafts destination preserving an important part of Asheville's history. In addition to the Antique Car Museum, the facility includes working artist studios, and the Biltmore Industries Homespun Museum remembering Asheville's weaving industry.

Antique Shopping

ASHEVILLE HAS TWO 'picking' and antique shopping areas. The first is the Biltmore Antiques District near the entrance to the Biltmore Estate, and the second is Downtown Asheville. The number one choice, hands down, for antique shopping is the Antique Tobacco Barn in the Biltmore Antiques District. The Barn, located at 75 Swannanoa River Road, has been voted best place to buy antiques in Western North Carolina with over 77,000 square feet filled with "something for everyone, whether you have a lot to spend or not." Originally, the building was used for tobacco auctions. You have probably heard the expression "stuff expands to fill all available space" That explains a lot about the Tobacco Barn—its sheer size and good prices make it the standout it is. The Barn is not for the ten-minute shopper. You will need to plan on investing an hour or more. One word of warning. The Barn is not air-conditioned and has only minimal heating. So, dress accordingly, bring a bottle of water, and wear comfortable shoes.

In addition to the Tobacco Barn, there are nine other outlets in the Biltmore Antique District:

- Biltmore Lamp & Shade Gallery: In addition to lamps and shades, the store located in the heart of Biltmore Village, has elegant antiques, accessories, and seasonal decorations.

- Village Antiques: Located at 755 Biltmore Avenue, the store carries unique period French furniture and art.

- ScreenDoor: The mall, at 115 Fairview Rd., has over 50 dealers with a mix of antique, vintage, and new items.

- Bryant Antiques: Located at 120 Swannanoa River Road. This mall hosts over 70 dealers with merchandise ranging from funky to fancy—estate jewelry, vintage clothing, sterling, objects d'art, ephemera, fine china, textiles, quilts, chandeliers, and furniture from primitive to Victorian.

- Oddfellows Antique Warehouse: Oddfellows carries a wide selection of hand-picked European imports to high quality mid-century pieces. It is located at 124 Swannanoa River Rd.

- Sweeten Creek Antiques: It is a 31,000 square foot browser's paradise located at 115 Sweeten Creek Rd. offering designer décor, vintage clothing, collectibles, kitchen memories, big toy collection, pottery, and art glass.

- Estate Jewelry Ltd: The 18 Brook Street store carries private owner and estate diamonds and fine jewelry.

- The Regeneration Station: This mega thrift store at 26 Glendale Avenue just off Swannanoa River Rd. has early, primitive, and midcentury modern antiques and upscale art.

There are three Downtown Asheville locations that deserve to be on your antique shopping list:

- Captain's Bookshelf: Located at 31 Page Avenue, the bookstore has been buying and selling secondhand and rare books since 1976. Their stock includes numerous signed books, first editions and fine leather bindings as well as a generous collection of quality secondhand material.

- Lexington Park Antiques: You will find this favorite mall with over 70 dealers at 65 W. Walnut St.

- Battery Park Book Exchange: Sip a fine wine or Champagne while perusing thousands of books in dozens of categories. The Exchange is located at 1 Page Avenue, Grove Arcade.

Apple Valley

JUST A SHORT drive from Asheville's downtown center, a mere 25 miles, are the stunning orchards and farms of Apple Valley. And most welcome visitors, offer tours and even let you pick your own apples right off the tree. Not many people realize that North Carolina is the seventh largest apple-producing state.

Over 40 varieties are grown in the Asheville mountains including favorites like Winesap, Honeycrisp, and Granny Smith. Different varieties ripen at separate times lengthening blossoming and harvesting times. Harvesting begins in early August and runs through October and as the apple season wanes the farms extend visiting times with pumpkins, gourds, and other fall produce. Most farms are open daily from August through November with some as early as June and as late as Christmas. Grandad's Apple farm is an example of those in the valley. It is located two miles from I-26 on US Highway 64 also known as Chimney Rock Rd. Once there, you can walk into the orchard and pick your own or just load up from the enormous selections of already picked apples. The fun does not stop there. Grandad's Barn and Country Store is full of fall harvest decorations, apple peelers, apple bakers and other apple gifts. You can enjoy turnovers, fried pies, apple bread, caramel apples, ice cream, cider and the list goes on.

At Stepp's Hillcrest Orchard (221 Stepp Orchard Dr., Hendersonville, NC) visitors can take a ride on the farm wagon on weekends through acres of orchard and Farmer Stepp's pumpkin patch. Stepp's is another opportunity to enjoy great apple products including fresh apple cider with a doughnut in the picnic area. Lyda Farms located at 3465 Chimney Rock Rd. in Hendersonville welcomes visitors from June through November. Sky Top Orchard in Flat Rock at 1193 Pinnancle Road is open August through mid-December. The farm sits atop Mt. McAlpine with panoramic mountain views, their 100-acre farm is a family fall tradition for area residents with wagon rides, bamboo forests, farm animals, and famous freshly made apple cider donuts! And, of course, apples on and off-the-tree. Barber Orchards at 2855 Old Balsam Rd., Waynesville is open August-Christmas Eve. Their bakery is a local favorite especially known for their apple turnovers, fritters, pies and more.

While not exactly an Apple farm, Hickory Nut Gap Farm is a fun stop and it's right on the way between Asheville and Chimney Rock, and it is open every day, year round. Visitors get to see animals raised in their natural outdoor environment—goats at play, pigs in the woods, chickens laying eggs, and cows grazing in pastures. Stop by their Farm Store for local honey, jams, and fresh farm products. Directions from Asheville: I-240 East, exit towards 74-A East, Bat Cave and Chimney Rock. Follow 74-A approximately 9 miles. Turn left on Sugar Hollow Rd.

Apple Ripening: Early August: Ginger Gold, Zestar; Mid-August: Gala, Swiss Gourmet; Late August: Honeycrisp, Golden Supreme, Ruben, Tsugaru, Early Fuji'; Early September: Jonagold, Golden Delicious, Red Delicious, Shuzuka; Mid-September: Cortland, Jonaprince, Mutsu, Fuji, Blushing Gold, Jonathan, Ultra Gold; Late September: Cameo, Red Rome, Stayman, Winesap, Crimson Crisp, Taylor Rome; Early October: Granny Smith, Winecrisp, York; Mid October: Arkansas Black, Braeburn, Pink Lady, Gold Rush, Nittany, Evercrisp.

Arboretum

IF YOU LOVE the outdoors—forests, gardens, and trails for hiking or pleasure biking, you are in luck. Asheville is the home of one of the most beautiful natural settings in America, the North Carolina Arboretum. Located in the Pisgah National Forest, it is 493 acres of crisscrossing forest coves and meandering creeks in the botanically diverse Southern Appalachian Mountains. The Arboretum was established under the auspices of the University of North Carolina in 1986 by the State General Assembly. But its beginning dates back over a hundred years to when Frederick Law Olmsted, American's father of landscape architecture, envisioned a research arboretum as part of his plan for the Biltmore Estate. The Arboretum is located just south of Asheville and adjacent to the Blue Ridge Parkway at Milepost 393.

The gardens and trails are open daily, weather permitting, 8 AM–9 PM from April thru October, and 8 AM–7 PM from November to March. The Education Center is open daily 9 AM–5 PM. The Center is also open from 6-9 PM on Thursdays from April thru-October. While admission is free, there is a parking fee.

Special events and tours are available and the best way to stay informed is to go to the website, https://www.ncarboretum.org/. During regular hours, visitors can enjoy more than 10 miles of dog friendly hiking trails that range from easy, to moderate, and difficult. Picnicking is also permitted on the grounds. No alcohol is allowed, so bring the cheese but leave the wine at home! You can also purchase picnic items at the Education Center which also houses the Arboretum's temporary exhibits and the work of regional artists. Or just stroll the 65 acres of cultivated gardens that delight the senses and showcase the region's rich cultural heritage. It begins with the Exhibit Center's small Baker's Garden, filled with colorful perennials. From there you make your way along the Grand Garden Promenade, a broad path through a series of meticulously maintained themed gardens:

- Blue Ridge Court: A central point of the Grand Garden Promenade and features a garden pool.

- Heritage Garden: The garden includes plants used in the region's medicinal herb and craft industries. The chimney and stone foundations and water spring are reminiscent of old homestead sites.

- Holly Garden: The garden hosts a variety of plants in the holly genus grown in the area.

- Plants of Promise Garden: Located along the woods' edge, the garden demonstrates landscape plants appropriate for the Southern Appalachian region and the use of stone.

- Quilt Garden: Enjoy this floral representation of a traditional quilt pattern from a stone overlook.

- Stream Garden: The garden features the communities of plants along Western North Carolina Mountain streams.

- National Native Azalea Repository: The repository features species native to the United States and was created to preserve and protect native azaleas.

Axe Throwing

HAVE YOU EVER wanted to throw an axe? Well, now is your chance! Asheville is home to "Axeville", an axe throwing club where you can learn, or practice your skill, throwing an axe (or hatchets, their smaller counterparts) at wooden targets. Axeville's location is only four miles from the downtown area. I should add, in addition to throwing axes, they also serve some of the best local craft beers, ciders and wine that Beer City, USA has to offer.

It seems that beer and axe throwing, like beer and darts, just naturally go together. However, don't think it is just for fun! It is a real sport—throwers are serious even with Olympic aspirations. The International Axe Throwing Federation (IATF) holds an annual championship with standardized rules and regulations. It is fun, however, and like bowling, there are both recreational and professional leagues.

Newcomers to axe throwing are always welcome at Axeville. Coaches are on hand to teach you how to throw and explain the formal rules of the game. How hard is it? In as little as 15 minutes, you can learn the basics and start competing with friends with Axeville coaches guiding you through the axe throwing experience from first throw to final score. Their coaches are also there to ensure the safety of the participants and guests. Nevertheless, as you would expect, the venue is adult only. You must be at least eighteen.

The Axeville Club is located at 99 New Leicester Hwy. Monday through Thursday are reserved for private parties and league play, but the club welcomes anyone on Fridays from 4:30pm to 10:30 pm, Saturdays from 12:15pm to 10:30pm and Sundays from 1:00pm to 6:00pm. They set up a satellite location inside the Brewery Taproom in Biltmore Village on Fridays from 4:00pm to 9:00pm and on Saturdays from 2:00pm to 8:00pm. You can book a throwing session online by going to https://www.throwaxeville.com/ although they do accept walk-ins, subject to availability.

Once you have learned the sport, you will discover that there are similar clubs in almost every city in the U.S.

Basilica of St. Lawrence

WHEN THE NEW construction by Rafael Guastavino and son was completed in 1909, it was dedicated as the Church of Saint Lawrence. Only later was the term Church replaced by the designation Basilica. Basilica is a special designation given by the Holy Father to certain churches because of their antiquity, dignity, historical importance or significance as a place of worship. Those same attributes also placed the site on the National Register of historic sites. The National Park Service's National Register of Historic Places describes the Church as follows:

The Spanish Renaissance Revival style Church of St. Lawrence contains no beams of wood or steel in the entire building, all walls, floors, ceilings, and pillars are of tile or other masonry materials. The center dome, which has a clear span of 58 by 82 feet, is reputed to be the largest freestanding elliptical dome in North America. The roof is tile with a copper covering. Special interior features of the basilica include a Spanish woodcarving dating from the mid-17th century that represents Jesus, Mary, and St. John at the Crucifixion; a 17th-century painting of "The Visitation" by Massimo Stanzione; stained glass windows taken from the church building formerly on this site; and 10 semicircular windows made in Munich, Germany, which depict scenes from the life of Jesus.

The Basilica of St. Lawrence was created in a time of wealth and prosperity for Asheville. The Basilica reflects that time and stands apart from the ordinary in both Art and Architecture. Architecturally, it is a testament to the skill of the master builder and architect, Rafael Guastavino, who constructed its freestanding elliptical dome without support or scaffolding, laying the tiles in open air as if shingling an imaginary dome in space, using only cement. The entire structure of the church is built with only stone, brick, and tiles. And as for art, you will need to see it to appreciate the statues, paintings and stained glass works of art. They are breathtaking and well worth taking the time to tour this historic site. The Basilica of Saint Lawrence is located at 97 Haywood St. It is open to the public; however, you are asked to call (828) 252-6042 or visit the church's website, (https://saintlawrencebasilica.org), for information on tours and services.

Bears

Approximately 8,000 black bears range around western North Carolina, and many of those make Asheville part of their meandering. They are often comfortable enough with their human neighbors to den inside the city limits. Just recently, one Asheville resident thought they had a raccoon in their crawl space. There was a persistent scratching sound from beneath the floorboards. The homeowner ordered a couple of traps, but when a big furry black paw poked out from the latticework, they knew their small "have-a-heart trap" was not going to do the job. One of Asheville's black bears had selected the homeowner's crawl space as its den for a nice winter nap.

Don't be surprised if you encounter one of the furry friends, we share our town with. In fact, we would be surprised if you did not. But you do need to be "bear wise". As accustomed to sharing their mountains with humans as they have become, they are still wild animals and can weigh as much as 600 pounds. And from the human side, as cute as those little cubs are, you can be sure they are under the protection of Mama bear who is always nearby. SO, LOOK, BUT DO NOT TOUCH!

Watching our bears from a safe distance, like people watching, is a favorite Asheville sport. However, if you are out in the open, the North Carolina Wildlife Commission provides these "bear wise" tips on what to do if encountering a bear:

- Do not approach the bear. Quietly move away and leave the area.

- If you are a safe distance away from the bear, make loud noises, shout, or bang pots and pans together to scare it away.

- Give the bear a clear escape route.

Asheville humans have adjusted their behavior to live happily with their bear neighbors—things like bird feeders or feeding pets outside are a "no no", and there are special practices concerning trash, garbage, and food scraps. Ashevillians love their bears but understand that safe co-habitation depends on each keeping their distance.

Biltmore Village

THERE IS SO much to do in Asheville that visitors can never see or do it all, certainly not in one trip. So, you might as well book the dates for your return visit to the city. Because when you head home, you will be talking about all the things you wanted to do and just did not have time for!

We know that most first time visitors have the Biltmore Estate at the top of their to do list. But do not overlook the Biltmore Village, located across from the entrance to the Estate.

The Village was originally a planned community for estate workers and was designed by world renowned architects as a picturesque residential community with the quaint atmosphere of an English community. The homes and buildings were built by the same talented artisans that built the Estate. The buildings are historic—constructed in the late 1890s. Today, it is a bustling shopping destination and home to some of Asheville's favorite restaurants. You will find one-of-a-kind shops as well as familiar national chains. Most of the businesses are in original cottages and buildings. The Village was declared a National Historic Area in 1989. The tree lined brick walkways and period architecture make for a delightful experience. There are more than forty shops and ten cafes and restaurants.

Don't overlook the side streets, like London Road and Reed Street, where you will discover remarkable finds including London District Studios in the emerging London

Entertainment District providing live music and several breweries.

Of course, shopping around Christmas time is a special delight as you probably figured it would be. On the first weekend in December, the community transforms itself into a Victorian age village with concerts, refreshments and strolling vocalists in period costumes. But you are likely to find things happening throughout the year. For example, in August it hosts its major outdoor arts and craft fair drawing thousands to the tree-covered grounds of the Cathedral of All Souls in the Biltmore Village.

Most shops are open Monday through Saturday from 10 am to 5:30 pm and Sunday from 1 to 5 pm. However, hours are usually extended for the holidays. But the restaurants are open for dinner—including Ruth's Chris Steak House, Village Wayside Bar & Grille, Fig, The Cantina, Red Stag Grill, and the Corner Kitchen. So, you can enjoy the wonder and ambiance of this transplanted Victorian English Village at night.

Biltmore Visit Tips

ALMOST EVERYONE VISITING for the first time plans to tour the Biltmore Estate. Taking in the Biltmore is not a couple of hours thing—it is a daylong activity. Reserve the entire day for your visit including lunch. And I suggest that you also consider having dinner there to close out your day at Biltmore. Amanda Williams is a long time travel reporter, and she published several tips based on firsthand experience:

1. Buy your tickets in advance to ensure you get tickets for the day you want. They sometimes sell out. There are limits on the number of people that can be on each tour. It also saves you from an extra stop since the ticket office requires you to pull over on your way into the Estate. Saving that stop also means you need to print your own ticket online vs. picking up a prepaid ticket.

2. Pay the extra fee for the audio guide. When you purchase your ticket, you will be offered several optional extras. The audio guide is one you do not want to pass up. It is only $12 per person, and it makes a big difference in the enjoyment of your visit. Your self-guided tour will keep you in the house for at least two hours.

3. Make lunch reservations. It is going to be a long day and you will not only want lunch you will need that break to rest your feet for a while. There are several options, but I suggest

The Stable Café. It is adjacent to the house, located in what used to be the old stables, and they serve up some good stuff at reasonable prices. And as Amanda notes, it is just fun to eat in an old, converted horse stable.

4. Go early. Biltmore sees more than one and a half million visitors annually. Your best chance of beating the crowds get there when the gate opens. Plan on having an early breakfast and then head to Biltmore so you arrive in time for the 9:00 opening. Being early also means you will likely get one of the parking places closest to the house. From there it is only a short walk (five minutes) to the house. Later visitors will have to wait on shuttles.

5. Book a Specialty tour. There is one extra that you cannot purchase online. Each day they offered a few special tours that let you access parts of the house that you cannot visit on the normal tour. They change from day to day. Amanda recommends stopping at the guest service booth next to the house when you first arrive to find the choices and that you book at least one of the extras. If they are offering the Rooftop Tour, I say grab it while it's available.

6. Visit the Gardens first. Amanda suggests at a minimum that you take in the Italian Garden, the Walled Garden with a walk through the Shrub Garden on the way. And be sure to include the Conservatory. The gardens close to the house are the most worth exploring.

7. Allow time to visit Antler Hill Village. This part of the Estate is about 5 miles from the house and has shops, craft demonstrations, an outdoor adventures center and an exhibition

about the Vanderbilts. For many, the most important reason for going to Antler Hill is the Biltmore Winery. That is where it is located. Your ticket includes a free wine tasting. You will have spent most of the day in the gardens and the house. Now after a little shopping and other Antler Hill activities, the tasting room is a great place to bring your long day of touring to a close.

However, before calling it day, I suggest that you have dinner in Biltmore Village just outside the Estate gate. The Vanderbilt's built the village to house the Estate's staff. Today, it is no longer a residential area. Instead, it has become a booming community of shops and restaurants. The entire area is a re-creation of a Victorian English Village and has been designated an Historic National District. For dinner there are at least ten alternatives to choose from including Ruth's Chris Steak House, Village Wayside Bar & Grille, Fig, The Cantina, Red Stag Grill, and the Corner Kitchen. If possible, get your reservation in advance to be sure you can get a table at your first choice.

Blue Ghost Fireflies

ALL MY LIFE I have been surprised by the annual arrival of our lightning bugs as we called them when I was growing up. Now days most people call them fireflies. They arrive like clockwork every summer so there is no reason for it to be a surprise, but it is, nevertheless. I suppose that is because their arrival is so sudden. One night they are not there and the next night those wonderful little sparkling yellow lights are decorating the night.

Scientists explain how it all works—the result of a mixture of oxygen with pigments, enzymes and a chemical called adenosine triphosphate that acts on uric acid crystals in the firefly's light producing cells. But theirs is a poor explanation for the wonderous sight as they arrive to light up the summer nights.

But Asheville cannot just have ordinary fireflies. The city that boasts that it is the weirdest, quirkiest place in America seldom does anything ordinary. For two to four weeks in late spring or early summer, several valley floors around Asheville are blanketed by the eerie blue lights of Asheville's Blue Ghost fireflies. Instead of the yellow lights we are used to, these fire-flies emit a unique blue-white hue, and the color is not the only thing different about the otherworldly version of our familiar lightning bugs. While ordinary fireflies flash on and off, the male blue ghost glows for up to a minute at a time--painting streaks of bluish light through the forest. The females do not fly, they crawl up on leaves and foliage and glow to help males find them, painting dots of blue along the forest floor. With countless meandering glowing fireflies, the forest floor becomes adrift with blue ghostly smoke-like wisps. As for why they are called Blue Ghost Fireflies, mountain legend held that the glowing blue fireflies were the ghosts of Confederate soldiers, as many lost their lives in the region where the fireflies appear.

Viewing this unusual firefly isn't easy. Because they prefer moist forest floors, people walking the trails in the area would likely crush them. That is why some areas close their trails during the Blue Ghost mating season to preserve these unique creatures. The Cradle of Forestry in Pisgah National Forest offers Blue Ghost Tours. Space is very limited. Online booking opens around the middle of April of each year. And while the dates vary, the tours are near the last half of May and the first week of June. For more information go to https://cradleofforestry.com.

Asheville Hiking Tours offers Blue Ghost Firefly Tours. Again, space is very limited. They start booking for Blue Ghost Firefly Tours in February of each year. Go to their website, https://www.ashevillehikingtours.com, for more details.

Botanical Gardens

JUST TWO MILES from downtown, the Botanical Gardens at Asheville is a beautiful spot for a leisurely stroll to enjoy nature. The Botanical Gardens highlight the ecosystem of the area. That includes native plants, some in danger of extinction, that have been saved and cared for in these gardens for more than 50 years. As one reviewer put it:

> We're reminded of how everything works together, including birds, pollinators, wildlife, soil, water, and air. Without any of these contributors, plants could not thrive. Without plants, humans could not thrive.

The garden collections focus on plants native to our Southern Appalachian Mountains and include a large variety of trees, shrubs, vines, wildflowers, herbs, grasses, sedges, aquatic plants, ferns, mosses, and lichens—approximately 600 species in all. You can enjoy this beautiful display while traversing the site's ten acres on an easy half-mile loop trail that takes you across bridges over streams, through meadows, and across a woodland ridge to a wildflower cove.

The peak wildflower season is April to mid-May; however, something is always flowering. berries and goldenrods are plentiful in Summer. Fall brings out the varieties of Asters and Eupatorium and the trees explode in a display of autumn colors. A winter's stroll will not disappoint you.

The Botanical Gardens are a great place for a picnic lunch. You will find strategically placed picnic benches and tables throughout. Regardless of the time of day, you will be surprised at how easy it is to spend quiet moments listening to the creeks ripple and the birds sing.

One of the most unexpected things in the Gardens is the "Moon Tree," grown from the seed of a tree taken on the 1971 Apollo 14 lunar mission. It is on the west end of the garden, near Weaver Creek. There is also Hayes Cabin, built in the 1840s and moved from Madison County to illustrate what life in the mountains was like in the early years. If you are visiting with children, pick up an investigation passport for each child. The passports send their holders on a mission to use their investigational skills to find historic markers, certain plants, trees, and garden locations that they then record in their passports.

The Botanical Gardens are open every day of the year from dawn to dusk. There is no fee for admission, although donations are always welcome. The Visitor Center, housing the Garden Path Gift Shop, is open daily from mid-March through mid-December.

Unfortunately, if you are traveling with your pet, you will need to leave it with a friend since dogs are not allowed.

Drum Circle

BOOMLA, BOOM—IF IT'S Friday night in April through October, you are in luck. Put on your dancing shoes or grab your drum or best people-watching attire and head for Pritchard Park in downtown Asheville on Patton Avenue at College Street. It should be easy to find just follow the sound of the drums—boomla, boomla, boomla—boom! and discover folks of every age and description dancing and swaying to the thunderous rhythm of the drums.

That's the location of the Drum Circle, a favorite Asheville tradition. The Drum Circle began in 2001 with 10 drummers. Since that time, it has grown into a community-wide event that includes all who want to join the fun. The Drum Circle has no leader or rules, which means everyone, regardless of race, ethnicity, age, gender, religion, or any other social identifier, is more than welcome to join in and feel the beat. The Circle includes percussion instruments of all kinds, including, congas, shekeres, djembes, dunduns, tambourines, triangles, and bells.

There is no better place or time to experience the individuality and diversity of this wonderful "weird" mountain city. Everyone plays a different role, from drummer to spectator, but that's just part of the fun. And the fun usually begins about six in the evening and builds until the end at ten at night. If you arrive early or decide to take a break from the beat of the drums, Pritchard Park is surrounded by Asheville restaurants, unique galleries and museums, and plentiful shopping opportunities.

I can promise you that a night with the Drum Circle revelers will just make you feel good!

Cheese Country

WHAT NAPA IS to wine, Asheville is to cheese. But Asheville does not forgo wine. In fact, you will discover that there are 20 wineries in the North Carolina mountains and foothills near Asheville! And they pair wonderfully with Asheville's native cheeses.

While you are enjoying your stay in Asheville, plan on spending an afternoon soaking in the mountain beauty while you sample some of the best handmade cheese being made in the South. Visit farms and creameries where extraordinary cheeses from goat and cow are crafted. Most have tasting rooms and many offer accompanying wines. Plan to buy some of your favorites at their source. Those lucky enough to be here during April can take advantage of the popular North Carolina Mountain Cheese Fest. The Fest features cheesemakers from the Western North Carolina Cheese Trail as well as other cheesemakers from around the Southeast. It is held during the month of April on The Meadow of Highland Brewing at 12 Old Charlotte Hwy, Asheville. Any time of the year you can create your own tour and tasting by visiting nearby locations. Here are my three favorites:

Looking Glass Creamery: This award-winning producer is an easy twelve-mile drive from downtown Asheville and is open Thursday through Sunday from 11:00 to 5:00. Get a bottle or glass of wine and one of their cheese plates to enjoy outdoors in their garden by the goats. Their creamery and Cheese Shop is located at 59 Noble Road, Fairview, NC 28730 on the way to Chimney Rock. Even if you don't have time for a lunch of wine and cheese, you can sample their cheese and hand-crafted caramel in the Cheese Shop where you will also fine local goods from nearby farms and food producers.

Blue Ridge Mountain Creamery: The next visit on your personal tour will be only seven and a half miles from Looking Glass Creamery if you put Blue Ridge on your schedule. However, it is down a curvy mountain road. The cheese maker, Victor Chiarizia, built his own cave for aging his cheese. He welcomes visitors by appointment on Wednesday and Friday cheese making days, so give him a call in advance at (828) 551-5739. Tasting tours are $5 per person. His distinctive cheeses are handcrafted in small batches and are cave-aged at a constant temperature. The Creamery is particularly noted for its Gouda and Blue Cheese. They are located at 327 Flat Creek Road, Fairview.

Round Mountain Creamery: Two creamery visits in one day are likely to be more than enough. So, you may want to save Round Mountain for another day or choose it in place of my other two recommendations. Round Mountain is about 25 miles from Asheville. Their 28-acre farm south of Black Mountain is home to 150 goats from which they produce twelve wonderful soft and seasonal aged goat cheeses. You can arrange to tour the milking and production areas and meet their friendly goats. Their store opens on Friday & Saturday from noon to 4:00pm. Call (828) 669-0718 in advance for a guided tour on Wednesday through-Saturday.

If you are traveling the Blue Ridge Parkway, consider following the Western North Carolina Cheese Trail. For a listing of all the creameries and a map of their locations go to https://www.wnccheesetrail.org/the-map.html.

Chocolates

THE ASHEVILLE AREA is not only the home of great wines and cheeses, it is also the location of a fantastic chocolate factory. Think about it! While visiting Asheville, you can spend a day in the tasting rooms of our local wineries, another enjoying the tasting rooms along the cheese trail and a third day at the French Broad Chocolate Factory & Tasting Room. What more could you ask for?

When Dan and Jael Rattigan met at a wedding in 2003, the course of each of their lives changed. They dropped out of graduate school, packed their lives into a 40-foot vegetable oil-powered school bus, and drove south to Costa Rica. There, they bought an abandoned cacao plantation and started on a very chocolatey journey that eventually brought the couple and their chocolates to Asheville where they first opened the French Broad Chocolate Lounge featuring their custom made chocolate and chocolate treats. You cannot miss it. If you go to Pack Square and see a long line of people, then you have found it, the French Broad Chocolate Lounge. It is a chocolate lover's dream where you will find a delicious variety of hand-crafted artisan chocolates and pastries featuring superb local and organic ingredients. The Lounge is a place where you can sip a glass of wine paired with your favorite chocolate or discover how a creamy stout brew pairs with vanilla ice cream and their dark, dense cacao brownie. The Lounge is located at 10 South Pack Square and is open late making it a top spot for dessert after dinner at one of the 50 downtown restaurants.

Another option is to tour their second location, the factory, where the magic happens as cacao beans are turned into chocolate. The French Broad Chocolate Factory & Café is located at 821 Riverside Drive, Asheville, NC 28801, just two miles from the city's center, the Grove Arcade. Tours are offered at 2pm and 4pm daily. The tour lasts about 45 minutes and includes a walkthrough where you can see each step of the chocolate making process. You will learn about the wonderful and sacred cacao tree; how farmers and producers grow, harvest, and process its cacao beans; and, of course, how the factory turns them into chocolate! According to The French Broad Chocolate website, their tour guides weave the story of French Broad Chocolate—from a magic school bus to a Costa Rican jungle café and then to the Chocolate Lounge & Chocolate Factory in the mountains of Asheville! And you get to taste the journey with a selection of their bean-to-bar chocolates. The tour and tasting prices vary but are usually $10.00 or less per person. To book your tour go to https://www.frenchbroadchocolates.com/pages/tours

Ashevillians love their chocolates and you will discover that as good as French Broad Chocolates are, they are not the only game in town. Others include the Chocolate Fetish at 36 Haywood Street, Kilwins at 26 Battery Park, and Asheville Chocolate at 25 Broadway Ave. The Fetish truffle bars are filled with layers of luscious Belgian chocolates. Their Ultimate Crunch Bar is a tantalizing mix of almonds, apricots, cranberries, hazelnuts, krispies, and pistachios in a blend of fine European chocolates. Kilwins is like a step back in time to an old-fashioned confectionary! And, Asheville Chocolate offers fine truffles and gelato, all made by hand in small batches in the shop.

City Hall

FOR ITS SIZE, Asheville has had more than its share of famous people. One was Douglas Ellington, an architect who put his lasting mark on Asheville as a master of the Art Deco style.

It was 1926 before Ellington arrived in Asheville to put his permanent stamp on the city's architectural character. Writing about Ellington's life, Dale Wayne Slusser wrote, "Douglas D. Ellington was born in 1886 in Clayton, North Carolina to Jesse & Sally Ellington. Ellington attended college at Randolph-Macon College, in Virginia and received his architectural training at Drexel University in Pennsylvania. In 1911 he went to Europe to supplement his education at the Ecole des Beaux-Arts. He completed his studies at the Ecole, just prior to the start of the First World War. After serving in the military in the 'camouflage unit' during the War, Ellington returned to civilian life and secured consecutive teaching positions first at Drexel, then Columbia University, and finally at the Carnegie Institute of Technology..."

Asheville was in a building frenzy in the 1920s' and was just the kind of avant-garde place for the buildings Ellington wanted to design. Unfortunately, Asheville's building boom ended abruptly with the Great Depression of the early 1930's. Douglas Ellington was forced to move on and while he continued to return to the city as a visitor, and to oversee construction of homes he designed for numerous Asheville individuals, he never again took Sky City as his permanent residence. But his impact lives on most notably in the Asheville City

Hall. Considered an Art Deco masterpiece, Ellington sought to capture the contours and textures of the city's mountain backdrop. He selected materials to match the clay-pink shades of Asheville's soil. Inside the City Hall you will find murals by New York artist Clifford Addams portraying stories of Native Americans and early white settlers in the region. Its fanciful nature and embellishments are in tune with whimsical Asheville. Five Ellington designed buildings remain in downtown Asheville as historic architectural landmarks: the Asheville City Hall, S & W Cafeteria, First Baptist Church, Asheville High School, and Merrimon Avenue Fire Station.

The architectural character of Asheville today did benefit from the Depression in one way. The earlier building boom had placed the city deeply in debt forestalling urban renewal projects that took place in many cities following the Depression and later periods—that consequence saved most of Ellington's masterpieces when many Art Deco buildings were being demolished and replaced by modern glass walled structures.

Asheville's architecture is unique not only for the contributions of Ellington but from many other extraordinary architects and builders— including many brought from around the world to create the Biltmore Estate. A must for visitors is the architectural trail through the downtown area of Asheville. For more information www.exploreasheville.com/architecture-trail/.

Cradle of Forestry

WHEN THE UNITED States Government established the 500,000-acre Pisgah National Forest, a 6,500-acre site was set aside as a National Historic Site to commemorate the beginning of forestry conservation in the United States and to tell the story of America's efforts to preserve its great forests. Today, that site is the home of the Cradle of Forestry and includes a reconstruction of the first forestry field school. The original Forestry School was established in 1898 by Dr. Carl A. Schenck, who had been hired by George W. Vanderbilt to establish the forest at his Biltmore estate. The original field school was in a community school and church in the Pink Beds community located deep in the Pisgah Forest. The community got its name from the blooms of its dense growth of rhododendron and mountain laurels.

Many of the old mountain cabins and farm homes within the Pink Beds community became the "campus" of the Biltmore Forest School. One building, a single-room community school and church, served as the forestry school's classroom. Seven of the historic buildings nestled beside an old sawmill and a 1915 Climax logging locomotive have been preserved and are on display at the Cradle of Forestry site. The exhibit hall displays forest history through interactive displays including children's games. There is an optional half hour film that tells the story of the birth of scientific forestry management. The exhibit hall includes a fire-fighting helicopter simulator that visitors can ride over a forest fire. The exhibits include an underground view of the animals and creatures that live under the forest floor. Don't leave the site, however, without also taking the one mile walk into the late nineteenth and early twentieth century to experience Appalachian Mountain life as it would have been during the period. All along the Cradle's Biltmore Campus Trail, visitors can interact with local crafters (woodsmen, quilters, basket makers, spinners, weavers, blacksmiths, and even toymakers) as they demonstrate the skills required for survival by the mountain residents. If you have worked up an appetite, you can return to the exhibit hall's café and visit the gift shop before returning to Asheville.

Why was this spot in the middle of the forest so important that it earned the named the Cradle of Forestry and was designated a National Historic Site? To understand that answer, we need to step back in time to the early 20th century. The Appalachian Forest, like many of the country's woodlands, were subject to devastating large-scale commercial exploitation. And deforestation for fuel was widespread throughout the nation. A concept of sustained management of woodlands was nonexistent in this country, but pioneering conservationists abroad were beginning to devise reforms for forest management. In 1889, George Vanderbilt hired a young European educated forester, Gifford Pinchot, to care for the vast woodlands around the Biltmore Estate. When Pinchot left to pursue his work at the national level, Vanderbilt hired a German forester, Dr. Carl Schenck, to replace him. It was Schenck, as noted above, who created the first school of forestry in America, the Biltmore Forestry School. The action of all three men, Vanderbilt, Pinchot, and Schenck, revolutionized the way we think of our woodlands and Schenck's advent of formal forestry training ignited the national movement toward sustainable forest by creating the educational discipline of forest management in the United States.

The Cradle of Forestry Historic site is located on US Hwy. 276 in the Pisgah National Forest only about 30 miles from the center of town, the Arcade Building. It is a four-mile trip from the Blue Ridge Parkway near Milepost 411.

Crossroads Monument

WHY IS THERE an Asheville? Before Ashville became a town, it was part of the Cherokee Nation. By the 1600s, some thirty Native American tribes lived in the valley, the Cherokee remained the largest. The town of Asheville was not settled until 1784. It was named for the revolutionary period Governor of North Carolina, Samuel Ashe. However, what is now Asheville had existed for centuries prior to the town's founding as a Crossroads. When early explorers like De Soto came to this area in about 1539, they followed well-worn Native American trails. And the spot now occupied by Pack Square was the location where two of those trails crossed.

For European settlers, native trails were their roads and highways. The Asheville Crossroads became a stopping place as they drove livestock to markets—including pigs, turkeys, and cows from Tennessee to markets as far south as Charleston. Movement of livestock and wares was mainly along the North-South leg of the trails and in 1827 the route became an actual road—the Buncombe Turnpike.

The Crossroads monument located in Pack Square marks the spot where the trails crossed—giving purpose to the area and leading to the birth of the city. The monument is a re-creation of the trail complete with footprints of Native Americans, booted drovers, turkeys, pigs, and cows. Steel rail borders on each side of the trail represent the arrival of railroads in 1880 that moved Asheville into the modern age.

The rails in the monument were reclaimed from the original Asheville streetcar systems.

Pack Square is located at the intersection of Patton, Biltmore, and Broadway in the Downtown Asheville Historic District. The square is host to free activities and festivals throughout the year. As one Asheville visitor put it, "Pack Square is quite simply the still beating heart of Asheville. It's a place to relax, people watch, grab dinner, dessert, have a coffee on a bench, or bask in the sun."

Cycling with Bears

SINCE MANY VISITORS to the mountains are avid cyclists, it is appropriate to bring to your attention one of the unique attributes of the Asheville area.

Asheville is a biker's paradise for both off-road and road cycling. And bicycles trump cars for getting around in downtown Asheville, but when you leave the in-town streets and head out for the open road, the Blue Ridge Parkway or any of the many biking trails, there is one thing different about cycling around Asheville—black bears. Yet, despite their daunting appearance, black bears pose little danger unless they're surprised. Fortunately, bear attacks are extremely rare, but you do need to be "bear wise". They are wild animals and can weigh as much as 600 pounds. So, LOOK, BUT KEEP YOUR DISTANCE! And never try to outrun a bear. Like dogs, they have a chase response, and they can sprint more than 30 mph.

REI co-op has a great website dealing with wildlife encounters while biking. Here is what they have to say about the subject of black bears:

The cyclist is usually the one at fault when an animal gets scared. Picture it. Here's some old black bear, hunting for berries and grubs when suddenly the flash of sun on metal and the sound of tires interrupts its rummaging. If it doesn't spot an immediate escape, it may believe it is trapped. And no creature likes to feel trapped. Your job, then, is to calmly allow the bear time to gather its wits and escape. This is tougher than it sounds. Your first reaction is the flight-or-fight syndrome. You want to avoid confrontation as much as the bear. The urge is strong to slam those pedals and spit flames from your tires to escape. Resist it. In most cases a bear can outrun you.

Instead, come to a stop. Start talking in a calm, clear voice. Talk about the nice bear and how you're sorry for interrupting its snack time. Get off your bike and position it between you and the bear. Either hold your position or start slowly backing away. Most black bears are happy to retreat quickly.

In some cases, the bear will rise up on its hind legs. This allows the bear to see and smell you better. A bear's sense of smell is one of the most acute in the animal kingdom, estimated to be 100 times more powerful than a dog's. Their eyesight has long been regarded as very poor, but that opinion is changing. It's a good bet that if you can see a bear, it can see you.

If the bear stands, just keep talking and keep backing away. If you can move uphill, do so. This gives the bear more opportunity to escape, as it will choose the path of least resistance. In still rarer cases the bear may lay back its ears, lower its head, make a "woofing" sound and open its jaws. It will look like a nose guard getting ready to sack the quarterback. It could be that you have come between the bear and her young. Bears sometimes make bluff charges. Stand your ground; don't "play dead" with a black bear. Don't run. Having your bike between you and the bear is still the best idea and can serve as a last line of defense. If the bear approaches, shout, make noise, stand tall, throw small rocks. If it makes contact, fight back vigorously. Ideally, you can give the bear enough room so it will leave before your confrontation escalates to this point.

Dog Welcome Center

ASHEVILLE IS HOME to the country's first official Dog Welcome Center, Dog City, USA!

It is more proof that Asheville loves dogs. The Welcome Center is a place where your dog can get a fresh drink of cooling water from its doggie drinking fountains, pick up a free dog goody bag and, of course, take advantage of its public restrooms and potty areas. While at the Welcome Center pick up information on the best dog friendly attractions, restaurants, and things to do. The Welcome Center shares space with The Dog Door, a canine shop full of treats, toys, chews, and dog necessities. The Dog Door and the Welcome Center, Dog City USA, are in downtown Asheville across the street from the Grove Arcade at 1 Battle Square. The Center is open Monday-Wednesday 9-5, Thursday-Saturday 9-7, and Sunday 11-5.

The Center operates tours designed exclusively for visitors and their dogs. The tour will take you to local shops with doggie goodies, breweries catering to pups, and restaurants that offer special canine dining for you and your dog. If you are interested in the unique dog-friendly experience, be sure to call (828) 656-8305 in advance to book your spot. The tours are conducted on Fridays at noon.

The Twisted Laurel restaurant downtown located at 130 College Street adjacent to Pack Square Park, dishes up a special menu for dogs bringing their owners to lunch and dinner on their dog-friendly outdoor patio. Features include the Twisted Doggy Bowl with a choice of protein—salmon, chicken, burger, or scrambled eggs. For dessert, your dog has a choice of doggy ice cream, restaurant made doggy biscuits, or frozen yogurt coated in peanut butter with a fruit center. The Twisted Laurel restaurant is open Tuesday through Saturday for lunch and dinner, as well as fresh craft cocktails, dozens of beers on tap, and an extensive wine selection that can all be enjoyed either inside in their spacious dining room or outside on their dog-friendly patio adjacent to Pack Square Park.

If you are not up for lunch or dinner with your canine companion, check out the Battery Park Book Exchange in Asheville's Grove Arcade. You and Fido can browse their 22,000 new and used books, or just head to the Champagne bar and order a glass of wine, a pint of beer, or an espresso paired with a cheese and sausage plate, a smoked trout dip, or a dessert to nibble on while you read. While you must pay for your drinks and snacks, your dog gets to eat and drink for free. It is a great place to spend an afternoon sipping and reading with your pet or for taking a short break from shopping.

Asheville boasts 81 other dog friendly activities in Asheville. For a list, including plenty of dog parks, go to the Bring Fido website for Asheville (https://www.bringfido.com/destination/city/asheville_nc_us/_).

Dr. Elizabeth Blackwell

ASHEVILLE'S 1.7-MILE URBAN Trail is a walk through Asheville's history. The walk is in five sections representing periods in the life of the city. Station #6, The Blackwell Memorial, is in the Gilded Age (1880-1930) section. You will find it on the side of the Wachovia Bank Building on Patton Avenue. It is a metal bower of medicinal herbs which houses a bench and head of Dr. Elizabeth Blackwell, a former Asheville resident. A pioneer in medicine for women and children, she was the first woman awarded a medical degree in the United States.

According to the accompanying plaque on the Trail, before enrolling in the Geneva Medical College in western New York, Elizabeth Blackwell began her medical studies in Asheville in 1845 under Dr. John Dickson. She had taught music at Dickson's private school for girls. The school was located on the site of the Drhumor building.

The bronze representation of Dr. Blackwell was sculpted by Jim Barnhill. The plaque and artwork were funded by the Buncombe County Medical Auxiliary and Buncombe County Medical Society.

Blackwell's career choice was remarkable in that at the time it was considered inappropriate for a woman. She was rejected by 29 medical schools before being admitted to Geneva Medical College in 1847. The faculty had been opposed to her application but decided to put the issue to student body and pledged to abide by their decision. Surprisingly, they voted yes. According to her biography on the website of Hobart and

William Smith Colleges, there are two possible reasons for the vote outcome:

Either the young men of the medical school thought that the members of the faculty were joking when they said that a woman had applied and so they joined in the joke by voting yes, or the students knew that the faculty was genuinely troubled and thought it would, therefore, be hilarious to vote to admit the woman applicant. In any event, from that supposed joke came Elizabeth's opportunity, which she seized with determination and ultimate success.

She graduated two years later, January 23, 1849, at the head of her class. Among others her accomplishments included:

- Authoring *The Laws of Life, with Special Reference to the Physical Education of Girls* in 1852.

- Founding the New York Infirmary for Women and Children.

- Starting the first Women's Medical College.

Fall Season

FALL IN ASHEVILLE explodes with color. We have over 100 species of deciduous trees. That, and our high mountain air, give the Blue Ridge Mountains one of the most vibrant and long seasons of fall foliage. Our fall color season usually begins in late September at the highest elevations and continues into the first weeks of November in the lowest elevations with their peak yellows and oranges in mid-October.

The Blue Ridge Parkway is a 469 mile scenic drive through fall's colorful show of reds, yellows, and orange. But you don't have to drive almost 500 miles for the colorful show. Visitors staying in Asheville's hotels or one of our bed and breakfast inns will find that the show is all around them. And if they want to take to their cars, there are ample nearby opportunities for hiking and panoramic views without venturing more than fifty miles away—including such scenic points as Glassmine Falls, Craggy Gardens, Mt. Pisgah, Folk Art Center, Chimney Rock, and the Fryingpan Mountain Lookout Tower. Each with trails for getting up close to nature with a walk amongst the falling leaves. However, don't overlook the North Carolina Arboretum or the Biltmore Estate. The Arboretum has over 10 miles of trails traversing its 434-acres. As for the Biltmore, a walk through its gardens will dazzle you with nature's show-case of colors.

One of the best ways to travel among the colorful fall land-scapes is by bicycle and if you didn't bring your own there are plenty of bike rental shops with both traditional and electric bikes. Some of the bed and breakfast inns, like the historic Applewood Manor, have a stable of all-road bicycles for its guests as a rental option. You can cycle around Asheville's downtown area and the Manor's historic Montford neighborhood, head out to one of Asheville's many bike trails or just take off for a ride through the mountains. The serious cyclist might head for the Elk Mountain Scenic Highway. This 60-mile route features continuous elevation gain, but rewards riders with stunning views of the Blue Ridge Mountains before reaching the Blue Ridge Parkway. Once you get there, you might consider continuing the Parkway up to Mount Mitchell, the highest peak east of the Mississippi River.

For the ultimate fall foliage viewing, consider a hot air balloon trip. It isn't inexpensive but if ballooning is on your bucket list, call Asheville Balloon Company at (828) 707-2992 or book a flight, from $300 to $400, on their website at https://ashevilleballooncompany.com/.

It isn't just foliage that brings people to Asheville in the fall. There is a feeling of electricity in the air. The change of season creates an excitement and explosion of energy that brings on festival after festival in Asheville and the surrounding small towns and communities. And then there is Halloween. Halloween events abound—some hauntingly frightening like those events and tours organized by Ghost Hunters of Asheville (http://www.ghosthuntersofasheville.com) and Joshua P. Warren's Grove House Ghost Hunt and others are entertainment and pure fun oriented—food, craft, and music events. Never forget that Asheville is considered one of the most haunted places on earth, allegedly fueled by its quartz laden mountains and the paranormal and energy vortexes in their valleys and mountain slopes. And locals will tell you that of all the places in Asheville none are more haunted than the

Montford Historic District—the perfect place for a walk or bike ride on Halloween.

Festivals and Events

IT IS ALMOST impossible to set forth a schedule of year round festivals, fairs, and events because new ones are always popping up in Asheville and surrounding towns. Despite the difficulty of the task, I have done it anyway. Here is my list (compiled from internet sources) of regularly scheduled annual events.

Asheville Art in the Park (www.ashevilleartinthepark.com) has booths featuring handcrafted art including glass, ceramics, wood, jewelry, and metal. It takes place on three consecutive Saturdays in the last half of June and three consecutive Saturdays in the early half of October in Pack Square Park.

Asheville Fringe Arts Festival (www.ashevillefringe.org) in mid-January focuses on unusual and alternative expressions of dance, performing arts, puppetry, and music. A pass for the festival will cost you $65.

Banner Elk's Small Town Christmas (https://www.bannerelk. com/latest-news/a-small-town-christmas) is held in the first week of December. The three day event starts on Friday with tree lighting, variety shows, farm tours, rides, etc.

Big Crafty (www.thebigcrafty.com) is a twice-yearly craft bazaar, with music and beer, held in early July at Pack Square Park and early December in the Civic Center. Admission is around $5 for adults.

Brevard Music Festival (www.brevardmusic.org) in the Brevard Music Center in Brevard from mid-June to early August present symphony concerts, chamber music and operas. Some events free, others various admission costs.

Brewgrass Festival (www.brewgrassfestival.com) is held at Salvage Station (468 Riverside Dr.) in early October. Featuring music and craft beers. Admission is $35.

Carolina Mountain Cheese Fest Asheville is held on The Meadow of Highland Brewing (12 Old Charlotte Hwy, Asheville) in April. The festival spotlights more than 20 local food businesses representing cheese, charcuterie, crackers, bread, chocolate, and more. Featured cheesemakers from the WNC Cheese Trail. For a small additional cost, enjoy pairings cheese with beer, wine, and hard cider.

Chow Chow Festival (http://www.chowchowasheville.com) is a culinary event series in August and September to celebrate the food of our Southern Appalachian region in in Pack Place Park and other venues around town.

Christmas at Biltmore from the last week of November through the first week of January you can see America's largest home decked out in all its festive finery. Evening's candlelight cast an almost magical experience.

Concerts on the Quad (www.unca.edu) held at University of North Carolina-Asheville, are a "bring lawn chairs or blankets and picnics" free concerts on several Mondays in June and July.

Craft Fair of the Southern Highlands (www.southernhig hlandhandicraftguild,org) fills the Civic Center with more than 200 talented craftspeople, members of the Southern Highland Crafts Guild. It is held twice yearly, in mid-July and mid-October.

Dirty Dancing Festival (www.dirtdancingfestival.com) it is a two-day weekend festival in mid-September. It is held at the site used for the movie *Dirty Dancing* at 2948 Memorial Hwy, Lake Lure, NC 28746.

Downtown After Five (www.ashevilledowntown.org), draws a big crowd for free local music. Takes place from 5-9 pm the third Friday of the month from May to September at the foot of North Lexington Avenue near the I-240 Overpass.

Downtown Asheville Art District Art Walks (www.ashe-villedowntowngalleries.org) are held from 5 to 8 pm the first Friday of the month from April through December.

Drumming Circle (www.ashevilledowntown.org), occurs every Friday night from about 7-10 pm April-October (weather permitting) at Pritchard Park downtown on Patton Avenue, is an authentic Asheville experience, with drumming and dancing.

Festival of Flowers at Biltmore Estate (www.biltmore.com), takes place in late March to mid-May. The event showcases tulips, azaleas, and other flowers in the Biltmore Estate formal gardens and on the grounds.

Fly Fishing Festival (www.greatsmokies.com) is held on a Saturday in early November in Bryson City. Hosted by Tuckaseegee Fly Shop, there are usually more than 20 vendors showing the latest in rods and other fly fishing gear.

Folkmoot USA (www.folkmootusa.org) features dance and folk music groups from different countries. It is held in downtown Waynesville during the last two weeks of July. Various admission fees.

French Broad River Festival (https://frenchbroadriverfestival.com) is an all-weekend festival featuring some of the best music in the area and a number of outdoor events in celebration of French Broad River. The festival takes place on the first Friday through Sunday in October at the Hot Springs Campground & Spa, just 45 minutes north of Asheville

WNC Garlic Fest (www.wncgarlicfest.com) is usually held the first Saturday in October. It features different varieties of garlic from various local farms. The venue is the So True Seed store at 243 Haywood Street, Downtown Asheville. Free.

Goombay Festival is an annual celebration of African and Caribbean culture. The weekend festival usually held in early September.

Grandfather Mountain Highland Games and Gathering of the Clans (www.gmhg.org) is held annually in mid-July. The event continues over four days on Grandfather Mountain with traditional Scottish Highlands music and Gaelic culture--dancing, piping, fiddling, drumming, athletic events, and sheep herding.

Greek Festival (www.holytrinityasheville.com) is held the last weekend in September to celebrate Greek culture, music, and food. The venue is the grounds of the Holy Trinity Greek Orthodox Church on Cumberland Avenue in the Montford Historic District of Asheville.

Golden Nugget Drop on New Year's Eve is held on Main Street in downtown Marion to watch the giant golden nugget drop into the 10-foot wide eatable donut that you get to sample after midnight. Many activities.

HardLox (www.hardloxjewishfestival.org) focusing on the Jewish culture and food is a one-day festival held on a Sunday in mid-October in Pack Square Park in Downtown Asheville.

Holiday Parade downtown Asheville usually on a Saturday in mid-November kicks off Asheville's holiday season with marching bands, floats, dance, and theater troupes, walking groups and Santa Claus himself.

Halloween Tours are the perfect way to explore Asheville's ghostly side. LaZoom Haunted Comedy Tour (https://www.lazoomtours.com/ghost-tours-asheville) will have you laughing and screaming! More serious are tours by paranormal expert and TV personality Joshua P. Warren (http://www.hauntedasheville.com). Haunted History and Murder Mystery Trolley Ghost Tour by Gray Line (https://graylineasheville.com/tours/ghost-tour) provides more than an hour of ghoulish delights across Asheville.

Lake Eden Arts Festival (LEAF) (www.theleaf.com) occurs twice a year on a weekend in mid-May and mid-October, on

600 acres at the former site of Black Mountain College near Black Mountain. In the tradition of Woodstock, the event usually attracts 12,000 attendees and features more than 50 musicians and musical groups, plus arts, crafts, and poetry. Tickets must be purchased in advance. Single-day adult passes are in the $60-$70 range and weekend adult passes are near $200.

LoveShinePlay Yoga Festival (www.ashevilleyogafestival. com) is held over four days in late July at Pack Square Park in Downtown Asheville. A pass to all events is $250 to $350.

Montford Park Players Shakespeare Festival (www.montfordparkplayers.org) produces six to seven different Bard's plays per season in Montford Park in North Asheville. Donations are welcomed. The season runs from April through September.

Mountain Dance and Folk Festival (www.folkheritage.org) is the longest-running folk festival in America, having begun in 1928. The three-day event featuring traditional Appalachian music, dance teams and storytelling is held the first weekend in August. The performances are indoors on the campus of the University of North Carolina at Asheville.

Mountain Sports Festival (www.mountainsportsfestival. com) features sports and music. Usually held on Memorial Day weekend in late May. Activity involves martial arts, disk golf, motocross, triathlon, kayaking, bike racing and 5K run.

National Gingerbread House Competition displays amazing gingerbread houses open for view at the Omni Grove Park

Inn Wednesday through Sundays from Thanksgiving to early January.

North Carolina Arboretum Festivals (www.ncarboreturm. org) has a variety of events throughout the year, including a weekend show on orchids in late March, a bonsai expo (mid-October), and Winter Lights Festival, in November and December with some 500,000 holiday lights.

North Carolina Mountain State Fair (www.mountainfair. org) continues for 10 days in early September at the WNC Agricultural Center at 1301 Fanning Bridge Road in Fletcher off I-26 near the Asheville Regional Airport.

North Carolina Apple Festival (www.ncapplefestival.org) celebrates Henderson County's position as the leading apple producer in the state. Held on Labor Day weekend in early September, the Apple Festival takes over Main Street in downtown Hendersonville, with music, craft booths, freshly picked apples, and cooked products like cider and apple pies.

Organicfest (www.organicfest.org) celebrates everything organic. It takes place in Pack Square Park on a Saturday in late August.

Polar Express Train (https://www.gsmr.com/events/polar-express/) of the Great Smoky Mountains Railroad runs from mid-November through December. The 1.25-hour round-trip excursion departs the Bryson City depot for a journey over the river and through the woods to the North Pole to pick up Santa.

Ramp Festival is one of the oldest festivals in Western North Carolina and exists for no other reason than to celebrate the odiferous mountain wild onion. But you will find plenty of food, as well as blue-grass and mountain music. It is held the first Sunday in May at American Legion Field, 171 Legion Drive, near downtown Waynesville.

River Arts District Studio Stroll (www.riverartsdistrict.com) is held the second weekend in November. The event includes some 300 artists and craftspeople in dozens of studios and galleries.

RiverMusic & Riverfest (www.riverlink.org) The festival is held in July at New Belgium Brewing at 21 Craven Street in West Asheville. Attendees celebrate the French Broad with local music, river rafting, an "anything-that-floats" parade on the river.

Santa on the Chimney (https://www.romanticasheville. com/chimney_rock_santa.htm) usually held on the first two Saturdays in December has Santa Claus readying himself for clambering down chimneys across the world by practicing on one of the biggest chimneys of all, Chimney Rock! Watch him scale the 315-foot monolith and enjoy other festivities.

Shindig on the Green (www.folkheritage.org) brings traditional mountain music and dancing to Pack Square Park in most Saturdays in July and August. Stage Performance start at 7 pm, weather permitting, but people start jamming an hour earlier. Bring a lawn chair or blanket.

Sierra Nevada Oktoberfest (www.sierranevada.com/oktoberfestnc) takes place on a Saturday in mid-October at the Sierra

Nevada craft brewery site in Mills River near the Asheville Regional Airport.

Village Art & Craft Fair (www.biltmorevillage.com) is held the first weekend in August on the grounds of Cathedral of All Souls in Biltmore Village.

White Squirrel Festival (www.whitesquirrelfestival.com) is held Memorial Day weekend in Brevard to celebrates the town's population of white squirrels. It has live music and a soapbox derby.

Woolly Worm Festival (www.woollyworm.com) is held the third weekend in October in the town of Banner Elk.

Flatiron Building

DOWNTOWN ASHEVILLE HAS been designated a National Historic District and the eight story 1927 Flatiron Building is one of its architectural gems. The triangular wedge shaped building is located at 20 Battery Park Avenue. It stands at the fork of Wall Street and Battery where it welcomes walkers to the tree lined lane of Wall Street, full of shops and restaurants radiating the best of Asheville's affability and charm.

The building's Beaux Arts detailing employed by the Flatiron's architect, Albert C. Wirth, was particularly popular in the U.S. during the period from 1880 to 1920. The building's ties to the past continue as one goes inside. Antique fixtures create a feeling of stepping back in time to the 1920s—a feeling reinforced by the still functioning "operator-run" elevators.

John Turk, Professor Emeritus, Youngstown State University, and vice president of the Western North Carolina Historical Association describes Wirth's creation as follows:

Asheville's Flatiron Building is unique. Architect Albert C. Wirth designed the building in the neoclassical style—a style influenced by the buildings of the ancient Greeks and Romans. Consequently, Wirth's building follows the format of a Greek column. The first two stories, sheathed in limestone and decorated with low-relief ornaments, form the base. The next five stories of unadorned brick form the column. And all the fancy dentil work and a brass parapet at the top form the capital.

Everything is in perfect proportion. Change one thing and the whole thing falls apart. Well, almost everything. To my knowledge neither the Greeks nor the Romans ever built a major structure in the shape of a triangle. I'm also guessing that neither the ancient Greeks nor Romans ever attached a three-level outdoor bar to one of their buildings. Too bad. They missed the chance to relax with an after-dinner drink and watch the sun set behind glorious mountains.

Things are about to change, however. The Sky Bar has closed as the building is slated to be converted to a 71-room boutique hotel with restaurant, street-level retail and commercial office space and roof top bar. How much of the interior's tie to the past will remain is unknown; although, the developers intend to restore it to its "original glory."

I was familiar with New York City's twenty-three floor Flatiron building before seeing Asheville's and had always thought that the name related to materials used in its construction, only to learn Flatiron refers to the shape. People gave these wedge-shaped triangle buildings the name "flatirons" because the shape reminded them of clothing irons of the period. That was all the inspiration local artist Reed Todd needed to create Asheville's Urban Trail Station #8, a gigantic old fashioned clothing iron, that memorialized the architectural Flatiron treasure. The popular spot is used for public musical and art performances and is a meeting place landmark. The big flat iron is so popular with Ashevillians that it has its own Facebook page.

Folk Art Center

IF YOU ARE interested in folk art and crafts, the place to go is the Folk Art Center only about nine miles from Asheville's Arcade Building. The Center provides an opportunity to learn about regional craft and to view the works of over 300 area artists—you can browse rotating exhibitions in several galleries and watch artists at work. The ground floor's Focus Gallery and Main Gallery feature various artists throughout the year, so there is always something new to see. The upstairs area includes 250 works from the Center's permanent collection with crafts dating from the 1850's. The Folk Art Center also hosts many events throughout the year and has an extensive library of craft books and videos.

The craft shop inside the Center is the oldest continuously operating craft shop in the United States, dating back to 1897. In addition to artwork, its offerings include studio furniture and one-of-a-kind home accessories.

The Center is Located on the Blue Ridge Parkway at Milepost 382 near the Parkway's intersection with Highway 70. The Folk Art Center is the most popular attraction on the Blue Ridge Parkway. Over 250,000 visitors visit it each year. The location also includes the Parkway Store with National Park souvenirs and travel information.

Admission is free. The center is open daily except for Thanksgiving, Christmas, and New Year's Day. Its hours are from 9 AM to 5 PM, January through March and from 9 AM to 6 PM, April through December. If you are inclined to stretch your legs a little bit, you can access the Mountains-to-Sea Trail from the parking area. There is also, a ¼ mile trail that is designated as accessible according to the Americans with Disabilities Act. The adjacent picnic area is a perfect place to have lunch if you packed one before venturing out for the day.

French Broad River

THE FRENCH BROAD River running through the center of Asheville has its headwaters high in the North Carolina mountains and flows 200+ miles to feed the Tennessee River and eventually the mighty Mississippi. It is allegedly one of the oldest rivers in the world, even older than our mountains. The most common Cherokee name for the river was Tah-kee-os-tee, meaning racing waters. The English called it the Broad River in its 1766 map of Indian Nations, but with the French occupying most of the territory in the 1700s, it became generally known as the French Broad.

The river provides a wide range of fun-filled opportunities to enjoy its offerings. Its waters range from rapids perfect for whitewater rafting and kayaking to flat smooth water perfect for paddle boarding, tubing, and float trips. There are a plethora of parks and access points for fishing, bird watching, picnics and hiking, etc. Visitors have easy access to outfitters and river event providers that quickly put you on the river for French Broad memories to take home with you. Here is just a sample:

French Broad River Outfitters: Located near downtown Asheville offering paddle board, kayak, canoe or tube rental and shuttles for a river adventure. Also, rent camping gear and book trips down the river.

Asheville Outdoor Center: Offers equipment (kayak, canoe, tube, or paddleboard), shuttles, and expert guidance at this one-stop shop. You'll end your trip at their riverside campus. Grab a beer at their taproom afterward!

Biltmore's Outdoor Adventure Center: Biltmore offers peaceful float trips down the gentle section of French Broad River through the Estate. Paddle with your guide in a raft or get in a single or tandem kayak for a self-guided trip. All trips depart from Antler Hill Village inside the Estate, so admission tickets are required. Trips offered April-October.

Southern Appalachian Anglers: Take a guided fly fishing or bass fishing trip near Asheville. Enjoy the Appalachian Mountains by boating and/or wading in North Carolina's stream-fed lakes and rivers. Beginners are welcome for this relaxing day on the water! Southern Appalachian Anglers will supply all equipment and plenty of expertise.

New Belgium Brewery: Tour the amazing brewery and sample beers while watching the action on the river. Walk or bike the new riverside greenway!

NOC's French Broad Rafting: Take a whitewater rafting trip, half-day of five miles with Class II-III rapids or a full-day trip with eight miles that adds river-wide Frank Bell Class IV rapids named after the 1923 canoer who lost his canoe to the eddying currents. It's family-friendly with no experience required. All trips are guided through a very scenic section through the Pisgah National Forest. Learn a little history and see wildlife. It's only 30-minute drive from Asheville.

Village of Hot Springs: Travelers have journeyed to the natural mineral hot springs about 36 miles north of Asheville since the late 1700s. Before that, the Cherokee Indians revered its magical, healing carbonated waters. Today, you can soak in the same water, naturally heated underground along a volcanic fault line to a perfect 98-102 degrees. Book an hour or two in a private tub by the French Broad River and watch your stress and fatigue melt away.

French Broad River Park: Keep it simple with a visit to the River Park at 508 Riverview Drive in Asheville with, open green space, old trees, picnic gazebos, greenway access, scenic river overlooks, plus small playground, restrooms, and parking. There is also an off-leash dog park.

Glass blowing

SOMETIME AROUND 3000 BC man discovered that sand could be melted. The liquid sand when cooled turn into glass. It is likely the discovery was made by potters since the process requires a high temperature like that of a potter's kiln. Glass blowing came later. It was invented during the Roman Empire in the first century BC. The first glass blowing workshops appeared to have developed in areas now occupied by Israel and Lebanon. Rulers so valued the secret of glass making that glassblowers were virtually prisoners—not permitted to travel. Penalty of disclosing their methods was death. The tools and techniques used have remained almost the same since the discovery of glass blowing. Molten glass is gathered at the end of a hollow pipe. The glassmaker blows through the pipe creating a pliable glass bubble that can be shaped by swinging, rolling, or blowing. Separately produced pieces can then be added by a process called welding—handles, stems, and decorations.

Ever wanted to blow your own glass? North Carolina Glass Center will teach you how to master this ancient art or you can watch experienced glass artists at work. Or you can just shop among the outstanding works of art produced on site.

The Glass Center is dedicated to education, exploration, and collaboration in all forms of glass. As a non-profit organization, they provide space and tools to anyone inspired to work in glass. That includes experienced makers or anyone who is touching glass for the first time. The center describes itself as a warm, positive, safe environment to explore their creative side and experience a material that can be transformative. Whether you want a small sample or an in-depth experience, they offer an array of educational options to explore that range from 30-minute workshops to full 8-week courses. The shops are open and viewable to the public, so if you do not have time for a hands-on-experience, you can view a class or demonstration!

This is what the Center's website has to say about their hours and public accessibility:

> *The North Carolina Glass Center is open 7 days a week from 10am to 6pm. Located in the heart of Asheville's River Arts District, the North Carolina Glass Center is surrounded by many fine artist studios and great restaurants. In addition to offering classes and demonstrations, we are proud to have nearly 40 artists that work out of our studio. Our gallery is free and open to the public and represents the work of our artists and instructors. This includes emerging, undiscovered artists, as well as artists that have been working with glass for over 30 years. You may contact us by calling (828) 505-3552*

Once you are in the River Arts district, you will be in the center of studios and galleries for over 200 working artists in virtually all medias, and there are local breweries for a taste of Asheville's local beers or restaurants for dining between visits to studios and galleries.

Halloween Room

THE BILTMORE IS America's largest home with 250 rooms, 35 bedrooms, 43 bathrooms and 65 fireplaces. Most visitors to the Biltmore Estate, however, never see a room which is not included in its 250 room count. It is a cavernous brick walled storage area deep inside the basement of the Biltmore referred to as "The Halloween Room" because those walls are painted with murals of witches, bats, black cats, wooden soldiers, and other eerie images.

For years, the unusual area went unexplained. Some thought it was used for a children's Halloween party in the 1920's, but recent research discovered that it actually was prepared in December, 1925 as the backdrop for a New Year's party thrown by John Amherst Cecil and wife, Cornelia Vanderbilt Cecil.

An avant-garde Russian cabaret and theatrical troupe called La Chauve-Souris, which translates to The Bat, toured America in the 1920's. Its abstract sets for the stage were designed by Russian artists, Sergei Sudeikin and Nicolai Remisoff. The show had great success and its fans apparently included the Cecils who by this time had inherited the Estate.

Biltmore historians found a theatrical program in the Estate records and discovered that the illustrations on the wall for the most part were recreations of the stage sets depicted in the program.

According to the Biltmore historian, Leslie Klinger:

The Charleston Daily Mail reported that 100 guests attended the Cecil's New Year's Eve festivities welcoming the year, 1926. One costumed attendee, local resident James G.K. McClure, recalled arriving in the basement of Biltmore with his wife Elizabeth, armed with a guitar and an old accordion, to find a room full of "all kinds of gypsy atmosphere such as cauldrons and pots and glowing fire ... all around." Enchanted by the unexpected theatrics, he wrote a detailed account of the holiday soiree to a friend, describing "a gypsy dance at Biltmore House which was the best party I have ever attended.

Hot Springs

WHILE SITES AND activities of downtown Asheville are enough to keep you busy without ever driving or cycling out of the city, Asheville is also a great base for exploring close by areas of Western North Carolina. Believe me, that could keep you busy for a lifetime. Take a twenty-five-mile drive north and you can drive through the main drag of Hot Springs, North Carolina unless, of course, you decide to stop there for a while, and you should. Hot Springs is located at the junction of the Appalachian Trail, which goes right through downtown, and the French Broad River. If you do stop, you are likely to hear music drifting from the open doors of Bridge Street taverns.

The small town is surrounded by the Pisgah National Forest and has become a hub for outdoor activities—rafting, hiking, and cycling. The provisioner, Bluff Mountain Outfitters, can supply you with all your needs for hiking or backcountry adventures. They even operate a shuttle service for pickups and drop offs along trails or the river. There are also several nearby concessions and outfitters offering kayaks, canoes, and tubes, with guided and self-guided trips. The French Broad near Hot Springs has everything from Class I to Class IV white water.

Or if you just want to visit, shop, eat and sip a beer, Hot Springs will surprise you with the number of eateries and taverns in the small city. And the romantic Mountain Magnolia Inn has an upscale restaurant with extraordinary views of the bucolic landscape.

But it isn't the food, rafting, hiking, or cycling that is the city's claim to fame. That comes from the hot mineral water that gave the city its name, Hot Springs. Travelers have made the trek to the natural mineral hot springs since the late 1700s. But as early as 5,000 years ago, Native Americans had already discovered the springs which they believed possessed healing powers. Petroglyphs are still visible on Paint Rock, a 107-foot rock cliff, that researchers believe the Indians used as resting place for prayer and contemplation on their way to the springs. The Cherokee Indians revered the magical, carbonated waters and sent their sick and wounded there to recover.

Today, you can soak in water from the same naturally heated springs—its water heated as it percolates up through warm rock to a perfect 98-102 degrees while collecting an abundance of healing minerals. The water then emerges to the surface along a volcanic fault line. Hot Springs Resort and Spa offers one- or two-hour sessions in a private tub by the French Broad River. Their hot tubs are sanitized and refilled before each use. And no chemicals are added to the mineral-rich water. Tubs are private in covered shelters in the woods that run along the river. Book in advance to be sure you get your desired time slot by going to https://www.nchotsprings.com/book-now/ or call (828) 622-7676. Their address is 315 Bridge Street, Hot Springs, NC 28743.

Hot Springs is host to several festivals throughout the year, but the best known is the French Broad River Festival held in October. It is an all-weekend event with some of the best music in the area and a number of fun outdoor activities in celebration of their beautiful river and setting. To reach the town take I-240 from the downtown area. Take exit 4A onto Highway I-26W and U.S. 19/23 North toward Weaverville. Go 8.5 miles until you see a sign that says Hot Springs 2nd right. Follow Highway 25/70 North about 28 miles to Hot Springs, North Carolina.

Immortal Image

THE ASHEVILLE URBAN Trail is a 1.7-mile self-guided walking tour through the streets of downtown Asheville where public sculptures tell the story of Asheville's history. Station #5 on the Trail is the "Immortal Image", a reference to the frieze of a face carved into the capital of one of the Drhumor building's columns.

Drhumor is pronounced as "drummer"; however, locals often call the structure the Good humor or Dr. Humor building. Built in 1895, it is thought to be the oldest standing commercial building in downtown Asheville. Architect Allen L. Melton designed the grand Romanesque Revival building, and Biltmore Estate stone carver, Frederick Miles, was commissioned to carve the remarkable limestone frieze above the first-floor exterior as well as columns and their capitals. The original owner was William J. Cocke, an attorney who studied at the University of North Carolina and at Harvard. The building is said to have been named for an Irish lake on which the ancestral home of the Cocke family was located.

Immortal Image is the carved face of an Asheville florist named Cyrus T.C. Deake, also called "Old Man Deake." Although he reportedly operated the florist shop with his wife and brother, he apparently had a lot of free time and spent it watching the stone carver as he worked on the frieze. Miles was so struck by the man's interesting countenance that he immortalized the image in his carvings. Deake was about 70 at the time his face was carved onto the Drhumor Building's frieze. He was described as a Santa Claus figure because of his white hair and beard, and his portly figure. He died on November 11, 1908 in Asheville, North Carolina and is buried in the Riverside Cemetery, final resting place of author Thomas Wolfe.

The stone carver, Frederick Bullen Miles (1860-1921), was born in Shaftesbury, England, son of a master builder who specialized in construction of churches. He was apprenticed as a stone carver and sculptor and attended art classes at the School of Art in South Kensington. Thereafter, he began work as an architectural stone carver in London. In 1892, married to Maud Squinnell, the family immigrated to Asheville, North Carolina where he was employed as part of a large field of artisans hired to finish out the Biltmore Mansion for industrialist George Vanderbilt. Miles, like many other Biltmore artists, landscapers, craftspeople, and architects, remained in Asheville to work on other commissions. He gained some degree of fame for his work in Asheville and other Southern cities. He died in Nashville, Tennessee and is buried in Spring Hill Cemetery.

While it is the Deake carving that is singled out for the Immortal Image, Miles's Drhumor Building work features several carved faces amid the ornate carved stone frieze featuring British royal lions alongside angels, mermaids, shells and other creatures from nature and mythology. While the other faces have been called allegorical, some in addition to Deake's, may have been those of other Asheville locals.

Miniature Golf

IF YOU ARE looking for a little family fun, there is nothing like miniature golf to get everyone laughing. You might be surprised to learn that miniature golf has been around for over 100 years. What makes it enduring is that it is a simple game which people can bond over while playing. It is easy to learn, easy to play—the perfect family-friendly recreational activity. You can play it competitively or just to enjoy the company of friends while you play. Either way, it is sure to provide you with an afternoon of fun

Here is a list of nearby courses:

Tropical Gardens Mini Golf is less than three miles from downtown Asheville. The 18 hole course is unique. You play through and around Flamingos, Elephants, Zebras, Volcanoes, Giraffes, and Waterfalls. Hours are usually 10:00 AM to 8:00 PM. [56 Patton Ave., Asheville, North Carolina 28806 (828) 252-2207 https://www.minigolftropicalgardens.com]

Lakeview Putt and Play is 18 challenging holes of miniature golf on a lush 1-acre course right on the waterfront at Lake Julian. The Lakeview course a short 10 mile drive from the center of town, the grove Arcade, and is landscaped with native plants and trees that provide a stunning backdrop for the course that includes waterfalls, streams, jump shots, keyhole drops, etc. Hours are usually 10:00 AM to 9:00 PM. [2245

Hendersonville Road, Arden, North Carolina 28704 https://lakeviewputtandplay.com]

Fireside Golf is home to Chip and Bogey, the two Nigerian Dwarf goats, who have taken up residence in the middle of the 18 hole mini-golf course! The fun filled course landscaping is Western North Carolina inspired. Fireside Golf is about twenty miles from downtown Asheville. Hours are 8:00 AM daily until dark. [485 Brookside Camp Rd., Hendersonville, NC 28792 (828) 698-1234 https://firesidegolfrange.com/minigolf]

Fantasy Golf & Game Room is about 35 miles from center city Asheville in scenic Maggie Valley. Its 18 hole course features waterfalls, a lighthouse, and a magnificent view from the 18th hole tower. [3659 Soco Road, Maggie Valley, NC 28751 (828) 926-8180 https://www.fantasygolfandgameroom.com]

MAGGIE VALLEY CARPET GOLF operates two 18-hole courses at its Maggie Valley location so there is usually little wait time before you are on the course and having fun! Hours are from 11:00 AM to 10:00 PM. Maggie Valley is about 35 miles from Asheville's Arcade building. [3054 Soco Road, MAGGIE VALLEY, NC 28751 (828) 926-3255]

Mining for Gems

READY TO GET your hands dirty and do something really different—like mining for gemstones and gold? If you are, you are in the right place for it! Within an hour's drive from Asheville's downtown area are some of the most important mining districts in the world. You can go home with a pocket full of real gemstones including rubies, sapphires, emeralds, aquamarine, topaz or even a gold nugget or prehistoric fossil. There are a lot of options. One, for example, is a half an hour away, near the entrance of the Pisgah National Forest, 3338 Asheville Hwy, Pisgah Forest. But the best for your mining adventure is probably Emerald Village, a scenic spot that is home to twelve different mines, where you can mine for gems and gold. The village is located at 331 McKinney Mine Road, Spruce Pine. It is open 7 days a week, but like most area mines is only open from April through October.

You will not need to bring a pickaxe. The mine operator has built a flume—a trough with a bench along its length through which water from a running stream is redirected to run through the flume. You load dirt into your screen-box (a wood sided box with a screen bottom). You let the water run through your screen box and wash away the mud to discover the treasure left behind—any of some 25 different gemstones. Mine operators are there to help with technique and identification. And best of all, you get to keep everything you find—no matter how valuable. Gems come in just about every color imaginable. rubies are silky red. sapphires are usually blue but can come in every other color. Garnets are glassy red, pink, or reddish brown. Moonstones have a flat box shape and are white or gray, as well as peach or chocolate brown. Quartz comes in clear colors like amethyst and citrine or sometimes opaque colors with mica flecks like aventurine. Quartz crystals are clear and smooth multisided. As for gold, I don't need to tell you what that treasure looks like!

Plan on making a day of it. In addition to mining work at the flumes, you can tour the actual mines dug into the mountain, visit exhibits and gift shops. Pack a picnic lunch to enjoy on the grounds. While you don't need a pickaxe or shovel, there are some things you should bring along for your mining work--Ziploc bags to hold your gems. No glass is allowed in the flume area. If you don't want dirt under your fingernails, bring along rubber gloves. And dress for mining—old clothes and tennis shoes or boots. They are likely to get muddy, so you may want an extra pair to wear in the car.

If you catch "gem or gold fever" and want more, there are still more mining opportunities. Here are a few:

- **Thermal City Gold Mine**: An authentic gold mine dating back to the 1800s gold rush. You can pan for gold and screen for gems, and you can even talk to a real prospector. They are open from March-October and are located 43 miles east of Asheville at 5240 US-221, Union Mills.

- **Elijah Mountain Gem Mine**: Gems include rubies, sapphires, emeralds, quartz crystals, citrine, amethyst, garnets, aventurine, sodalite, opal, fluorite, aquamarine, and others. Their flumes are covered for mining rain or shine. The mine is located thirty miles from the center or Asheville downtown area at 2120 Brevard Rd, Hendersonville.

- **Gem Mountain**: Gems include emeralds, aquamarines, moonstones, garnets, citrine, amethyst, rubies, sapphires, and others. Fresh materials are brought fresh to the flumes daily. It is an hour's drive from downtown Asheville at 13780 Highway 226 South, Spruce Pine.

- **Gold City Gem Mine**: Their claim to fame is the 1061 karat sapphire discovered there! In addition to mining gems, you can pan for gold. Gold City provides an optional inside heated flume for cold days. The mine is an hour's drive from Asheville at 9410 Sylva Rd, Franklin.

Motorcycle Museum

JUST 30 MILES from center city Asheville, in nearby Maggie Valley, is one of the country's most unique museums, Wheels Through Time. It is a 38,000 square foot building with the feel of an old garage. It is dedicated to the preservation of American motorcycling history and the evolution of the motorcycle.

Over 350 of America's rarest and most historic classic motorcycles are on display in the museum. The machines represent 25 different brands, including icons like Harley-Davidson and Indian as well as gems of the past, including Excelsior, Crocker, Henderson, Pope, Yale, Crocker, Flying Merkel, and many more. And all the machines on display are in operating condition. But it is not just a timeline of machines on display. Motorcycling is a spirit—a brotherhood and sisterhood, a tight knit community bound together by a love of machine and the open road. There is something very American about the relationship between motorcycle and rider and between the rider and the likeminded community of bikers.

The museum has several lifelike exhibits. For example, there is a replica of an actual small town motorcycle shop. The Shop was the pride and passion of a young entrepreneur who came back from the great war with the desire to own and operate his own Harley-Davidson dealership. Shops like this popped up in small towns across the country. These independent dealerships were heavily involved in racing and local club activities. Many formed their own clubs, enabling a sense of not only customer loyalty but more importantly brand loyalty. Wheels Through

Time is not just a display of machines as impressive as they are. It is packed full of motorcycle memorabilia including works of the renowned artist, David Uhl, famous for his motorcycle related pieces. His paintings on display in the museum capture dynamic facets of the early motorcycle era and the beauty of these remarkable machines.

While Wheels Through Time is first and foremost all about the motorcycle and the biker community, it also includes an impressive automobile collection including a pair of 1932 roadsters, Packards and Lincolns from the classic era as well as distinctive "one off" autos such as a 1949 Veritas and the massive 1915 Locomobile built during the gilded age of American history.

The museum is a non-profit organization financed by tax deductible donations and annually holds a motorcycle raffle, which helps them continue their mission. For example, the 2021 motorbike raffled was a milestone 1948 Harley-Davidson Panhead finished in brilliant black and chrome brought back to life in the Wheels Through Time restoration shop. Wheels Through Time is located at 62 Vintage Lane, Maggie Valley, North Carolina 28751. And you can learn more about the museum by going to https://wheelsthroughtime.com.

Mountain Golf

THERE ARE MORE than 40 championship golf courses in Western North Carolina. Most are less than an hour's drive from downtown Asheville. In the late 19th century, visitors began escaping the heat of Southern summers by retreating to the mountains and they brought their golf clubs with them. While summer is still the best season for golf, golf enthusiasts made the happy discovery that mountain golf is a four season activity.

In addition to spectacular scenery, mountain golf courses provide a unique playing experience with tight, narrow fairways that follow the undulating curves of our Blue Ridge Mountains. Some of our courses open to the public include the following:

The Omni Grove Park Inn Golf is a 6720 yard par 70 course. **Golfweek** magazine listed the Grove Park Inn course in America's Best list (290 Macon Ave., Asheville, NC 28804-3711, (800) 438-5800).

Asheville Golf Course is a 6440 yard par 72 course. Five minutes from downtown, this public course is one of the oldest in Western North Carolina and is on the National Register of Historic Places. The course was designed by famed course architect Donald Ross in 1927 (226 Fairway Dr., Asheville, NC, 28805-2409, (828) 298-1867).

Black Mountain Golf Course is a 6215 yard par 71 course. Just seventeen miles east of Asheville, the course is home of the famous 747 yard, par 6, 17th hole—at one time the longest hole in the world (17 Ross Dr., Black Mountain, NC 28711-2862, (828) 669-2710).

Broadmoor Golf Links is a 6921 yard par 72 course. Broadmoor is nineteen miles to the south, just past the Asheville Regional Airport (101 French Broad Ln., Fletcher, NC 28732-8648, (866) 578-5847).

Reems Creek Golf Club is a 6492 yard par 72 par course. Located 8 miles from the center of Asheville, the course designed by Hawtree & Sons opened in 1989 (36 Pink Fox Cove Rd., Weaverville, NC 28787-9735, (800) 406-3936).

High Vista Golf Club is a 6936 yard par 72 course. Ten miles from the center of town, the course was designed by Tom Jackson (88 Country Club Rd., Mills River, NC 28759-2603, (828) 891-1986).

Springdale At Cold Mountain is a 6812 yard par 72 course. Only 17 miles from downtown Asheville, the course was designed by Joseph Holmes (200 Golfwatch Rd., Canton, NC 28716-5659, (800) 553-3027).

Cummings Cove Golf & Country Club is a 6,400 yards par 71 course. Designed by Robert E. Cupp, ASGCA, the course is 20 miles from Asheville's center of town (20 Cummings Cove Pkwy., Hendersonville, NC 28739-8711, (800) 958-2905).

Mural Trail

THERE IS AN official Appalachian Mural Trail that covers historical murals in North Carolina and Virginia. The trail map and mural details are laid out on the website https://www.muraltrail.com. Six of the historic public murals are in downtown Asheville, most within easy walking distance of each other. As you plan your stay in Asheville the Explore Asheville website, https://www.exploreasheville.com, suggests that your plans include a mural hunt—a cultural treasure hunt throughout the city's historical streets! When you reach one of the sites on the Mural Trail, take a "selfie" in front of the mural, upload it to the Mural Trail website at https://muraltrail.com/cgi-bin/upload-photo/ and receive a free tee shirt that says: "I hiked the Appalachian Mural Trail."

You will find the first mural, Golden Threads, at Pack's Tavern located at 20 S. Spruce Street. Muralist Doreyl Ammons Cain's work celebrates mountain music and the Shindig on the Green. The Shindig takes place in Pack Square Park on Saturdays from late June through early September each year. The free music and dance event starts about sundown and usually ends around ten at night.

Next is the Haywood Street Fresco. It is located at the United Methodist Mission Congregation at 297 Haywood Street. The lead artist Christopher Holt's fresco portrays Jesus's most enduring sermon, the Beatitudes, where he begins, "Blessed are the poor." On weekdays, you can view the fresco when the church is open, from 9:00 a.m.-3:00 p.m. To find the schedule for a viewing on a weekend, consult the Mission's website, www.haywoodstreetfresco.org.

The third mural on the trail is the Chicken Alley Mural, a 200 square foot art piece with a 10-ft. rooster designed and painted by Molly Must. Located at 4 Woodfin Street, the mural interprets the history of the chicken-processing plant for which the alley is named and the area's rich agricultural heritage. Chicken Alley is also known for the alleged ghost that haunts it. You will read more about Chicken Alley and its ghost in Part Three, *Paranormal Events, Mysteries, and Ghost Stories.*

The fourth is the Lexington Avenue Gateway Mural, a 3000 square foot mural underneath the Interstate 240 bridge over Lexington & Broadway Avenues painted by 6 different artists. It depicts a stylized timeline of Western North Carolina history. There is also an extension of the mural by Molly Must and Ian Wikinson of two men playing chess that depicts the image of two men who were real life daily regulars who played chess in Asheville's Pritchard Park.

Asheville's fifth mural on the Historic Mural Trail is the Triangle Park Mural, a 1300 square foot memorial to Asheville's Black History. The mural spans the two sides of Triangle Park, at the intersection of Sycamore Alley and South Market Street in downtown Asheville. This is the center of "The Block," an historic area that was the cultural and economic center of Western North Carolina's African-American community. The mural was a community project involving nearly 100 volunteers.

Number six and the most recently added is the Dolly Parton Mural located at 783 Haywood Road, the Beauty Parade Salon. The Appalachian Mural Trail honors the historic roots of mountain people and events. And Dolly Parton's rise from an Appalachian poor girl upbringing to her mega star status makes her the perfect ambassador for that mission. The artist, Gus Cutty, who works only with spray can paints, recently added another face to the mural, that of drag queen TV star, RuPaul, with Dolly's hair style.

While the above six are all the Asheville murals on the official "Appalachian Mural Trail", it is by no means all of Asheville's public murals. The rest won't earn you a T-Shirt, but they are sure worth extending your mural hunt to include them! Here are a sample of Asheville's other murals:

- The Last Drop of Wine by Jimmy O'Neal, located at 5 West Walnut.

- Daydreaming Woman on the side of Aloft Hotel at the corner of Lexington & Aston.

- Tribute to the Big Lebowski at Sky Lanes Bowling, 1477 Patton Avenue.

- Wild West Asheville at The Odditorium Bar, 1045 Haywood Road.

- Hall Fletcher Elementary School Mural by Ian Wilkinson and Alex Irvine, 60 Ridgelawn Rd.

- Good Vibes Silo at 1 Roberts Street and the continuously changing canvases throughout the River Arts District.

Many of the murals are the work of multiple artists and community volunteers. With so much talent and an enthusiastic community, murals and publicly approved graffiti projects continues to make Asheville more and more colorful.

Musical Heritage

MUSIC IS AN inseparable part of Asheville life. You find it everywhere and especially in its many festivals. As the saying goes, people in Western North Carolina can always find a reason to have a festival and you cannot have a festival without music. And while its cultural diversity promotes every musical genre, there is an unmistakable foot stomping Appalachian Mountain Sound—folks just call it "Mountain Music"!

And Asheville is home for two musical events that celebrate and preserve that traditional Mountain Music of the Southern Appalachian Mountains--Shindig on the Green and the Mountain Dance and Folk Festival.

Saturday nights in July and August are The Shindig on the Green Nights. That is when people dig out their musical instruments or dancing shoes and about 7:00pm head for Pack Square Park in front of Asheville's County Building. Come experience traditional music and dance t of Southern Appalachia. Some go just to listen and watch as volunteer professionals and amateurs perform on stage. Others will join one of the many ad hoc jamming sessions that spontaneously pop up in the park in the hour preceding stage performances. Some will be enjoying a picnic dinner. For those that did not pack a picnic basket, there are plenty of food vendors and nearby eateries. But mainly, everyone is there just to enjoy the beautiful music and dance traditions of Southern Appalachia on a summer evening in the mountains. The Shindig is a free event organized by the Folk Heritage Committee who select performers and bands from those offering to perform or from jamming sessions. Performers are limited to two songs, dances or storytelling insuring variety.

If you enjoy The Shindig on the Green, you will love its sister event, The Mountain Dance and Folk Festival. Started in 1928, the annual three day event, is the oldest gathering of its kind in the nation providing a platform for the talented of the traditions of Southern Appalachia high country. The festival is held on the first Thursday, Friday and Saturday of August with a different line-up of authentic bluegrass music and dance each night. Performances are in Lipinsky Hall on the University of NC-Asheville campus, 300 Library Lane, from 6:30-9:30 PM each evening. What will an evening at The Mountain Dance and Folk Festival be like? It will be an evening filled with the hand-clapping, foot stomping rhythms of Bluegrass, the high energy of clogging, plus Mountain Smooth Dancing and colorful storytelling. The songs and dances shared at this event stretch across time from the Scottish, English, Irish, Cherokee, and African heritage found in the valleys and coves in the Blue Ridge Mountains.

You can find more about the Folk Heritage Committee at https://folkheritage.org.

Pinball Museum

LOOKING FOR SOMETHING different to do? I suggest a unique museum—The Asheville Pinball Museum. It is, as SmokyMountains.com puts it, a museum where you can not only look, but you can also touch, play, eat and drink! One reviewer wrote:

> *A day's worth of Fun! This place is so much fun! We went expecting to only spend an hour or two but ended up spending almost an entire day!!!!! Great beer selection, staff was friendly, decorations are on point (even in bathroom) and there are not only pinball games but also old school arcade games (dig-dug, PacMan, etc...) and old school Nintendo games. We had so much fun!*

The museum is home for vintage pinball tables to admire and play. Each pinball table, some of which date back to the 1940s, features a plaque containing its date of production and its place in pinball history. The early machines were flipper-less with just a silver ball bouncing around some bumpers. As a result, many localities banned the machines as simple gaming devices. Flippers were added in the late 1940s and winning or losing became a matter of skill. Still, it took almost thirty years for the bans to be lifted and for pinball machines to become universally legal.

In addition to pinball, there is an arcade in the rear of the museum that houses a collection of original Golden Age

Arcade Cabinets that are maintained in working order, with plaques indicating each game's significance in the history of gaming. You can play more than twenty old school games like— Donkey Kong, PacMan, Ice Fever, Addams Family, Star Wars, X Files, Star Trek, and more.

The Museum is in the old Battery Park Hotel, one of Asheville's buildings on the National Register of Historic Places. It was built in 1924 as a replacement for the original Battery Park Hotel, a Queen Anne style beauty that was torn down to make way for the current 14 story tower. Today, the hotel's upper floors serve as housing for seniors with commercial and restaurants on the lower floor. There is no charge if you just want the museum experience, but if you want the hands-on experience of actually playing the machines, the fee is $15.00 for adults. For children, the fee ranges from no-charge to $12.00 depending on age. There is no need to bring your quarters with you because the admission package gives you unlimited play. And there are sodas and beer as well as snacks to make your play time reminiscent of time spent when the machines were in your local soda shop, pub, or hometown arcade.

The museum is closed on Tuesdays. Their hours of operation vary from day-to-day as follows: Monday from 1pm to 6pm, Wednesday, Thursday & Friday from 2pm to 9pm, Saturday noon to 9pm, and on Sunday from 1pm to 6pm. All children 12 and under must be accompanied by an adult and dogs are not allowed. The museum limits the number of players on the floor. Once they reach maximum occupancy, just like your favorite restaurant, you go on a waiting list to be called when space becomes available for your party. For information check out the Museum's Facebook page. One final note, if you are looking for that perfect conversation piece for your home, some of the machines are for sale.

Radio Museum

THERE ARE THREE million Amateur Radio Operators worldwide. Seven hundred thousand of those are in the U.S. And
they love to combine their hobby with travel. The Blue Ridge
Mountains are just the kind of place that attract these radio
enthusiasts. The mountains provide the height for their radio
signals to reach places in the country and the world still on
their bucket lists, and Asheville is the perfect home base while
in the area.

Radio operators are always interested in the history of
their hobby and the development of radio technology. They
are always looking for the opportunity to meet other "Hams"
and share stories about antenna design, equipment and radio adventures including volunteer assistance and message
forwarding during emergencies and disasters. That makes
Asheville a natural destination for "Ham" Radio Operators.
There are several Amateur Radio Clubs in the area. One of
the most active is the Blue Ridge Club open to all persons interested in Ham Radio communications. They meet monthly
(except in December) on the first Tuesday of each month in
Jackson Park at 7:00pm. The meetings are held at 801 Glover
St., Hendersonville about a 30 minute drive from the Grove
Arcade Building. It is a large brick house above the tennis
courts. Meetings cover a wide range of radio topics. As they
put it from A-Amperes through Z-Impedance.

Another reason Asheville is a vacation target for amateur
radio enthusiasts is its Radio Museum. The museum is only

three miles from the center of town, located on the campus of Asheville-Buncombe Technical Community College, Room 315, in the Elm Building on Victoria Road. Over 100 vintage amateur and commercial radios are on display and the museum tells and illustrates the story of early experiments and eventual commercialization of the technology—the internet of its time. There is an artistic side to the museum—exhibits of beautiful wooden cabinets, displays of luxury and glamor, as radios arrived in homes. On the educational side, the museum includes demonstrations of how radio waves work. For the novice there is the hands-on opportunity to beep out their names in Morse code, hear old radio dramas on period radios and see a live demonstration of a spark transmitter, the earliest wireless device for sending and receiving messages.

Radio technology continues to take us into the future. Many of the devices now in common use exist because of that technology even though the user probably doesn't realize it. Cellphones are two-way radios. GPS systems and Bluetooth devices are radios utilizing electromagnetic waves. It is radio waves that connect us to wireless internet routers, open car doors with key fobs, etc. The radio enthusiasts who maintain the museum have done a great job with the facility and with their website, https://www.avlradiomuseum.org/, that invites visitors (licensed radio operators or not) TO EXPLORE THE MAGIC OF RADIO WAVE WIZARDRY!

Rat Alley

OFF THE BEATEN path is another historic Asheville landmark—
a semi-underground landmark. It is Rat Alley, and it is usually
included in any discussion or speculation about subterranean
Asheville—the rumored tunnel system that conspirator buffs
allege was used for illegal smuggling of liquor during the prohibition years as well as for drug deals, prostitution, and other
sordid happenings.

Rat Alley is located under Wall Street and runs behind
some of the shops and restaurants on Patton Avenue. Some
have suggested that it served as a connector or transfer point
between various businesses and the more extensive subterranean tunnel systems that is said to crisscross the city. For
example, one branch of the tunnel system led to the brothel
below the Langren Hotel (Circa 1912) before it was demolished in 1964. The Pack's Tavern spur served as the supply
conduit for illegal liquor and moonshine. Longtime Asheville
residents say that an extensive tunnel also ran down Charlotte
Street, its exit now covered over by the Martin Luther King
ballpark. There are numerous reports of sinkhole openings
that exposed other segments of tunnel works below the streets
and buildings of the city.

Whatever glorious or notorious role Rat Alley once played,
it has since fallen on hard times. Author Marla Hardee Milling
writes of the time she stole her way into the tunnel-like covered
alleyway.

I wasn't quite sure how to access it, but as we walked into a parking lot past Jack of the Wood, I spotted the chain-link fence covering the entrance to Rat Alley. The doorway, propped open by an orange traffic cone, seemed to beckon us inside. We inched into the darkness, glancing over our shoulders and giggling at our willingness to venture into an area we were not sure if we should enter: Dim overhead lighting cast and eerie shadow over the chaotic assembly of trashcans, mops and empty beer kegs.... While I wish I could say it was more exotic in nature, Rat Alley is primarily a dingy storage area. While it does run underneath Wall Street, it's really not an underground tunnel. It is as its name reveals: an alley.

The Jack of the Wood restaurant mentioned by Author Milling is an Irish public house offering handcrafted ales, local sourced pub food and live music. The restaurant is located at 95 Patton Ave and the parking lot she refers to is just west of the Jack of the Wood building.

While Rat Alley may not warrant being on your "must-see" list for an Asheville visit, it was an important feature in Asheville's history. That makes it something you need to know about to be considered "Asheville Smart."

River Arts District

JUST EIGHT MINUTES away (1.5 miles) from Asheville's city center, the Grove Arcade, is the extraordinary River Arts District, or RAD as locals have started to call it. Two square miles of river front abandoned factories and warehouses have been reborn and repurposed into a center for creative arts. This phenomenon was not an accident. It was a convergence of several factors. It started with the 1970 Clean Water Act that led to restoring the health of the river water and the development of the French Broad River Park & Greenway Systems. It also grew out of the need for Asheville's growing population of artisans for a place to create, show and sell their work products. Artists needed cheap rent and large spaces. Even then, one more factor was needed to make the River Arts District work as a destination—planning and community support. It was the entire community—the citizens, Asheville government, foundations willing to provide financial support, and corporations that would donate land and property. They all wanted to make the River Arts District work. RAD has blossomed into a vibrant center of art, creativity, commerce, entertainment, and dining fueled by the energy and creativity of its inhabitants.

To best understand RAD, I suggest you visit their website, https://www.riverartsdistrict.com/. Here is an overview from the website:

The River Arts District consists of a vast array of artists and working studios in 23 former industrial and historical buildings spread out along a one mile stretch of the French Broad River. This eclectic area is an exciting exploration of arts, food, and exercise. Plan on spending a day or more visiting artists working in their studios, grabbing a bite of local cuisine or a brew and taking time to find art that's perfect for your world. More than 200 artists work in paint, pencil, pottery, metal, fiber, glass, wax, paper and more. As unique and individual as their art, so too are their schedules. There are no official "Open Hours" for the River Arts District, but at any given time throughout the year, you will find a plethora of open studios and galleries. If you are coming to see someone in particular, your best bet is to check in with them before your visit. Do it here, online via our search feature, or check the Studio Guide. Come be inspired, shop, meet the artists and watch live demonstrations! Some studios also offer classes and internships. See the individual studio websites for more information.

Take advantage of ample parking and hop aboard one of our free trolleys running on Second Saturdays and throughout the Studio Stroll Weekend. Well-behaved dogs are welcome, as well, in most studios and even on the Saturday trolleys! Come for the opportunity to take home that special artistic treasure made and sold by the artists you meet here. Start your collection today!

Rooftop views

MANY VISITORS HAVE fallen in love with Asheville and make it their regular vacation spot or even decide to stay and make it their home. When spending an evening in one of our rooftop restaurants or bars, it is easy to see why. The views of our mountains and city lights from these high top perches make a convincing argument for making one of those choices. Here are some of our best sky high places to enjoy the view.

Pillar Rooftop Bar is on the top of the Hilton Garden Inn at 309 College Street in the heart of downtown Asheville. Given all the live plants and greenery and fire pits, locals refer to it as the botanical rooftop. The menu is limited to small bites and dips, salads, and burgers but the cocktails list is lacking nothing, and the southward views are awe inspiring. Retractable garage doors connect the outside to a comfortable modern bar with great atmosphere and local, live music.

The Hemingway Restaurant and adjacent 4000 square foot rooftop patio of the Cambria Hotel at 15 Page Avenue evokes the flavor of Cuba with a mural depicting a Havana bar called the Floridita, a haunt of the famous author. It looks down on the Grove Arcade and downtown Asheville, with the beautiful mountains as their backdrop.

Capella on 9 in the AC Hotel by Marriott is one of the best views in Asheville. And while you are falling in love with our mountains and city skyline, you can enjoy tapas, cocktails, wine, and beer. It is sometimes windy on this ninth-floor rooftop so bring a jacket on cooler days and find a place near one of the fire pits. The hotel's address is 10 Broadway Street.

Montford on Top is the rooftop bar at the Double Tree by Hilton located at 199 Haywood Street. Locals say: "Come for the views and stay for the food and cocktails." My favorite is their local cheese and charcuterie plate. An express elevator takes you directly to this rooftop restaurant at on the corner of Montford Avenue and Haywood Street. The restaurant opens to a tiled veranda with couches and communal high-top tables.

The Edison at the Omni Grove Park Inn has one of the best patios in Asheville. While it is not a rooftop, its position on the side of Sunset Mountain affords stunning views of the city. There are a lot of seating options, and the menu is varied. But locals suggest that it is a great place for a burger and fries while enjoying its million dollar view.

Antidote is atop a real gin distillery, Chemist Gin. Actually, the distillery located at 151 Coxe Avenue also makes a great single malt whiskey. Before going legit, the founder, Debbie Word, learned the ropes at a small family still and from many hours of moonshining with her chemist daughter, Danielle. Their rooftop bar has a big-city vibe and pre-Prohibition feel with nooks and private places for avoiding teetotaling do-gooders and prohibitioners, but my choice would be the roof-top patio extension of the bar with its view of the South Slope, especially as the sun is setting. While we are speaking about distilleries, The Thirsty Monk at 92 Patton Ave is a another one with a rooftop patio bar. It is called Top of the Monk. It is not one of the tallest, but its height still provides a panoramic view of the majestic mountains surrounding the city. The Monk's claim to fame is its whiskey list and craft cocktails, both classic and modern, made with hand-crafted ingredients.

One way to experience Asheville's rooftop scene and perhaps make new friends is to book a seat on Asheville Rooftop Bar Tours, www.ashevillerooftopbartours.com. The most popular is The Rooftop Sunset Tour. Whichever tour you choose, you will spend three hours divided between three rooftop bars. The stops on the tour change regularly, but you can count on a premium tour that captures spectacular views of our city and historic landmarks all while enjoying sample drinks at reserved seats.

S&W Building

THE THIRTY STATIONS (stops) along Asheville's Urban Trail are a walking tour of the city's history. Station #7 is the 1929 S&W Building—an Art Deco masterpiece designed by the same architect, Douglas Ellington, who gave the city its art nouveau City Hall building. Ellington's remarkable designs were influenced by his time in Paris at École des Beaux-Arts. The S&W building was the home of the elegant S&W Cafeteria that for almost half a century was the place to be seen in Asheville. Unlike modern cafeterias, the S&W's ornate interior and white linen and china service was quite upscale. Times changed, and in 1974, the cafeteria served its last customer in downtown Asheville, relocating to the city's new mall. But the three-story building with its front facade sheathed in grey ashlar featuring polychrome ornamentation and exotic stylistic motifs continued to be regarded as an important architectural showpiece for Asheville. In 1977, it was listed on the National Register of Historic Places.

The grand old property is getting a new life as a dining and event hot spot in the Asheville Historic District. Two nephews of Douglas Ellington have reopened the property as the S&W Market. The revamped interior evokes the energy of the original cafeteria, but white linen and china have given way to a food hall format where diners can select from a host of different independent restaurateurs. The main level offers seating for up to 65 guests and standing tables for another 20. There are 100 seats on the mezzanine and an outdoor patio accommodates 40. The facility includes five thousand square feet that has been set aside as private event space accommodating up to 150 people. The event area, named Circa 29, has its own bar and has a speakeasy-style and vibe.

The current restaurateur lineup brings some of Asheville's best street food into an astonishing restaurant setting and includes:

- **Bun Intended** with a Thai street food menu with dishes like Hickory Nut Gap pork belly bao and build your own bowls with traditional sides including som tum salad and larb gai with minced chicken and sticky rice.

- **Buxton Chicken Palace** with their iconic fried chicken sandwiches.

- **Farm Dogs** featuring local grass-fed hot dogs, handcrafted sausages, and locally-make pretzels.

- **Peace Love Tacos** serving taco salads, street corn, nachos, all with responsibly sourced meats and vegetables, and of course, their famous tacos.

- **Times Bar** serving up creative seasonally inspired craft cocktails and coffee.

- **Highland Brewing Company** with a lineup of Highland's small batch and barrel-aged beer and a quick-serve bar.

- **Hop Ice Cream** with its homemade dairy and vegan ice creams, classic milkshakes, sundaes, desserts, and made-from scratch waffle cones.

The S&W Market is located at 56 Patton Avenue in downtown Asheville. Weekday hours are 11:30 a.m. to 10:00 p.m. and Sunday from noon to 8 p.m. The hours may change with seasons. And the restaurant lineup or menus are likely to evolve over time. For the latest, check the website www.swmarketavl.com.

Sister Bad Habit

ASHEVILLE HAS BEEN called many things—weirdest, happiest, quirkiest place in America, Santa Fe of the East, New Age Capital of the World, Beer City USA, Most Haunted and others. It has earned every one of those names and wears them proudly. If you don't believe me, drop into any one of the city's tourist shops and you can buy a T-shirt bearing your favor moniker for this crazy old mountain town whose energy vortex draws visitors from around the world.

You never know who you will see or meet walking the streets of Asheville—rich man, poor man, bohemian artist, eccentric billionaire, a professed warlock, or witch or even a man in a nun's habit.

Sister Bad Habit is a celebrity character often sited around Asheville. The "nun's" image is a favorite for T-shirts, scarves, and other apparel in Asheville's shops. There is even a locally crafted beer named after the nun. She, or he that is, is none other than Jim Lauzon. Jim and his wife, Jen, are the owners of LaZoom Tours. The pair were crazy-in-love street performers who bought a bus, colored it purple and pursued their wacky dream of offering entertaining tours of their zany hometown. LaZoom has grown to encompass three buses, four drivers, one director, eight guides, and more nuns than you can shake a ruler at! But LaZoom is still Jim and Jen's baby they write the scripts and play the comedic roles for their hilarious tours.

Keep your camera handy, because you just might catch a glimpse of Sister Bad Habit—riding by on a bike or just drinking a local beer.

If you are interested in having ninety minutes of fun and belly-laugher while learning about Asheville's history and discovering some of its hidden gems, you can book a tour by going to www.lazoomtours.com or calling (828) 225-6932. You might decide to go back to LaZoom for their two-and-a-half-hour "Fender Bender" tour to as they say, "*Hop aboard LaZoom's Purple Bus and rock out with a local band while we take you on a journey to Asheville's premiere local breweries.*"

Stepping Out

DESPITE WHAT TODAY we would consider primitive living conditions such as the lack of plumbing and dirt roads, in 1879 "high society" still flourished. And when people went to the theater, they did so in style. The Urban Trail memorializes the arrival of theater in Asheville with Station #3 titled "Stepping Out". The artwork consists of a top hat, cane, and gloves, cast in bronze to recall the theaters and the Grand Opera House that once flourished along Patton Avenue, making this hilltop street the early center of commerce and culture.

Think what it would have been like to live in Asheville in the 1800s. Keep in mind that most of the things we use today had not been invented or if invented had not reached homes, businesses, or the individual. Radio broadcasting did not begin until 1920 and the percent of homes with a radio did not reach 60% until 1930. Silent movies begin arriving in 1880. It was 1927 before we had talkies. And TV did not begin showing up in homes until 1950. But people wanted entertainment. Their answer was an Opera House. Every town of any size had to have an Opera House. Traveling performers put on live productions.

From the mid-1870s until about 1915, any building used for presenting entertainment on stage was usually called an "opera house." The term lent an air of respectability to the act of play-going. Despite its moniker, the attractions, as they were usually called, were hardly Grand Opera. *The North Carolina Historical Review* includes the following:

The Carolina Citizen on April 17, 1879 reported that the third floor of the Courthouse at Pack Square was leased for a first-class theatre that will be fitted up in handsome style.

On May 6 and 7th Thorne Company again presented two pre-opening performances with *Ten Nights in a Bar Room* and *Rip Van Winkle*. Then the new Opera House was formally opened on Tuesday June 3, 1879 with *Fanchon the Cricket*. Before the performance Miss Bonnie Meyers of the Thorne Company made a dedicatory speech.

The Grand Opera House was only the beginning of Theater in Asheville because once movies were invented, movie houses to show them streamed into the city. The Strand Theatre, at 17 Patton Avenue, was opened August 2, 1915. It was renamed State Theatre on February 14, 1934. The 'Strand' name was later used on the theatre located at 36 Biltmore Avenue, now known as the Fine Arts Theatre, which is the only cinema still operating in downtown Asheville. The Imperial Theatre, at 32 Patton Avenue, followed opening in 1922 and closing in the late 1970s. Two years later, January 12, 1925, the Plaza Theatre, located in the heart of downtown Asheville in Pack Square, opened with Douglas Fairbanks in *The Thief of Bagdad* and operated until the 1980s. Other downtown theaters followed only to be demolished in the 1970s including the Vance, Princess and Paramount Theatres. The last to close, the Imperial, was demolished in 1980.

The "Stepping Out" monument at Station #3 was created by students at the University of North Carolina at Asheville under the leadership of Professor Dan Millspaugh.

Tiny Doors

As a visitor to Asheville, you will quickly come to recognize that the town has a unique, funky quality, and the City's public art certainly makes that point. While some was done by named artists and some of that was paid for by the city, a bit here and there was contributed by unknown artists. One such piece is on the base of a building #3 on Woodfin Street between Lexington and Broadway. It is a series of tiny little "mouse" doors. The doors vary in height from a foot to a foot and a half. They first appeared sometime around 2014 and no one has ever taken credit for their arrival. As to who was the artist, it's a mystery, like many other Asheville mysteries.

The "mouse" doors are quite popular, and they tend to pop up all over social media including pinterest.com. Who knows, maybe the mice were trying to get into Chicken Alley right next door, between buildings #3 and #4. There were a lot of good things in Chicken Alley for a hungry mouse. But the alley is now known as one of Asheville's most haunted places. That scary place is the subject of another story—one in Part Three of this book titled, of course, Chicken Alley.

Trains

IT WAS THE coming of the railroads that opened Asheville to the country and later the world as a major tourist destination. So, it is only fitting that it should have its own railroad company, Craggy Mountain Line, Inc.—even if it is just for fun.

Craggy Mountain Line, Inc. is a non-profit organization which was formed in 2001 to acquire the last remaining three miles of the Craggy Mountain line, an historic section of track that was once part of the former Southern Railroad located in Woodfin Township. The organization's mission is to preserve the railroad in an operable state and open it to the public. That includes acquiring and restoring antique railroad equipment for use and display. They maintain a museum for railroad memorabilia and information about the history of the line and its significance to the development of the area. And they do all of that relying on volunteers.

Craggy Mountain Line makes regular runs at 4:00 PM daily from their 111 North Woodfin Avenue station to the end of the line and back, 3.5 miles, a 7 mile round trip. The ride lasts about an hour and 15 minutes. Tickets are $10.00 per person. In addition, they do charter runs and offer special seasonal runs around Christmas holidays and the fall color season. There are two versions of their charter runs. The standard is to the end of the line and back—a seven mile trip. The second is a two mile run to the Woodfin Riverside Park and picnic pavilion and a return after park activities. The pavilion can be rented in three hour blocks. Individual families as small as two people can join an existing charter run. For reservations or to find out the current schedule for their regular run call (828) 808-4877. You can learn more by going to their website www. craggymountainline.com. The station is only about 4.4 miles from the center city Arcade Building—a mere seven minute car drive.

Wake Foot Sanctuary

DOWNTOWN ASHVILLE IS a walking town. There is too much to see and too much to do for cruising by car. A bike is great if you know where you are going but to explore the city nothing beats shoe leather. But what do you do when your feet start telling you they have had enough? There are plenty of bars, beer halls, restaurants, and snack bars where you can take a load off and rest those feet. But for the serious explorer, there is a way to put life back in those tired dogs of yours. It's called the Wake Foot Sanctuary, and they are located inside the Historic Grove Arcade at 1 Page Avenue, Suite 115.

It is the perfect way for Asheville visitors to end a long day of walking—a place where you can take off your shoes and socks and slip your weary toes into a warm foot soak. While you are relaxing, you can enjoy a selection of tea varieties and nibble on French Broad truffles and shortbread cookies. The emphasis is on relaxation. It starts with a comfortable armchair and a heated neck wrap and then the entree--an intoxicating soak of essential oils, nourishing clays, and revitalizing salts for your tired feet. All their foot soaks are a warm and relaxing 45-minute experience. You select from a menu of handmade choices:

- Hit Refresh—Grapefruit, rosemary, fennel, and pink clay.

- Good Vibes—Sensual and sexy scents of vetiver, patchouli, and added coconut oil.

- Meditation Garden—Juniper, cinnamon, clary sage, and peppermint-based über-relaxing soak.

- Lavender Chamomile—The relaxation duo. Sudsy & fragrant, topped with dried flower petals.

- Old #9—Wintergreen and rosemary team up with our Signature Wake salts.

- The Clay Bath--White-clay, avocado, fennel, and clary sage make this soak velvety smooth.

- The Melt—Super moisturizing citrus ginger with coconut oil; herbal, carrot, and neem oils.

- Tea Tree & Mint—Tea Tree oil, peppermint, and avocado oils with green clay.

- Salty Beach Rose—The Salty Beach Rose soak of Lavender, jasmine, and detoxifying rose salts.

- Signature Soothe—Healing for the skin and muscles with oils of lavender, tea tree, & clary sage plus detoxifying Epsom salts.

While you are pampering your feet, consider doing the same for your head, neck & shoulders, or the hands & lower arms by opting for the add-on massage service from their licensed massage therapists.

Space is limited and demand is high, so it is always a good idea to call. And you can book ahead to reserve your spot. Call (828) 575-9799. You can learn more and find prices on their website at https://wakespa.com/.

White Horse

THE SPIRIT AND music of the mountains is alive and well at the **White Horse** music and arts venue located in the town of Black Mountain. The White Horse facility is as unique as the small town in which it is located. The White Horse building is a converted Chevrolet dealership in the center of the Black Mountain township. Don't let the township part fool you— Black Mountain is within the metropolitan area of Asheville, only about fifteen miles from the Arcade. The mountains of Western North Carolina are full of music and stories, and the White Horse provides a place to showcase and preserve them. It is a family friendly listening venue, where people can see and hear music and watch live performances. This is not a honky-tonk or late-night bar. In fact, performances start around 7:30 or 8:00. The emphasis is strictly on listening to music. And while mountain music is an important part, White Horse embraces all genres, spoken art and other live entertainment— including classical music, Jazz, Blues, Bluegrass, songwriters, Native American performers, poetry, storytelling and more. Their 16-foot-wide screen and High-Definition digital projector is used to show films and video content to enhance live performances. While the emphasis is listening and watching performers, they do have bar service and snacks—serving fine beers on draft and bottled as well as a selection of fine wines, soft drinks, coffee, and tea.

The town of Black Mountain is a great place to spend a day. Downtown streets are lined with independent shops, restaurants, art galleries, artisan eats, music halls, and breweries. There are over 40 shops, 30 restaurants and three breweries— food, both in-doors and sidewalks, plus art, crafts, and music. And the town enjoys typically mild weather year-round even in winter. The town is surrounded by the towering beauty of North Carolina's Black Mountains. I fell in love with the little town the minute I spotted all the rocking chairs scattered throughout the place—inviting visitors and consummate rockers like me, to sit a spell and enjoy the scenery.

The town's arty twist is not an accident. It was home to the Black Mountain College from 1933 to 1957 when the college closed due to funding problems. In its time, it was one of the most highly respected and innovative experimental art colleges in the U.S. The college and renowned faculty attracted creative and talented artisans from across the country who began to move to the region. Its influence lives on today and Black Mountain remains an artist's mecca. While the school only remained open for 24 years, its influence on American arts and crafts has been profound. In 1993, The Black Mountain College Museum + Arts Center opened in downtown Asheville to preserve the important legacy of the college. Even if you never make it to the town, don't miss the opportunity to visit the museum at 120 College Street.

Wildlife Park

IF YOU ARE staying in one of Asheville's many bed and breakfast inns, native black bears often drop by for a visit. If one of our wildlife neighbors stops by on your visit, remember to watch from a safe distance. If you haven't had that pleasure yet and want to visit up close with one of our friends or other of the native species of animals in our mountains, the Western North Carolina Nature Center is only a little over six miles from center city Asheville. The 42-acre wildlife park is home to over 60 species of wildlife that live or have lived in the southern Appalachian Mountains.

Most of the animals have been permanently injured or have been imprinted, meaning they have no fear of humans and never learned the skills they would need to survive in the wild. Others have never known a life in the wild at all or are endangered species that are part of a breeding program to ensure that we have a sustained population of endangered animals and can conserve them for future generations. The Center provides you with the opportunity to learn about the natural history of each species and the unique biographies of the wildlife that call the Nature Center home.

American black bears, despite their name, are often brown, tan, or even white. While generally shy and reclusive animals, they are quite innovative, and like humans they eat both plant and animal food. In the wild, they forage for grasses, fish, berries, fruits, nuts, insects, small rodents, birds, and eggs. Their intelligence, however, makes "bear-proofing" a serious task for local homeowners who often unwillingly share their garbage, pet food and even bird food with their black bear neighbors. Two of our bears, Uno and Ursa, live at the Nature Center:

- Uno was born in the wild during January, 2004, but he was removed from the wild at a young age for unknown reasons. Because he had imprinted on humans, he cannot be returned to the wild. Uno likes to play in his pool, run around his habitat or climb its structures and trees.

- Ursa was born in 2001 and, like Uno, was removed without learning survival skills. She was named for the Ursa Major family of star constellations, which is Latin for great bear. Ursa keeps her distance from Uno during the summer, but the two share a den together in the winter.

Some of the other creatures you will have the chance to see up close include the endangered American red wolf, river otters, Angora goats, the barn owl, a black rat snake, the elusive bobcat, corn snakes, Cotswold sheep, a cougar, the Eastern box turtle (the state reptile), a coyote, an Eastern screech-owl, a gray fox, gray wolf, Great Horned Owl, the least weasel, Nigerian Dwarf goats, Oberhasli goats, a red panda, red-tailed hawks, donkeys, Elvis the Skunk, rattlesnakes, turkey vultures, white-tailed deer and more—including Meatloaf, the Hellbender. Hellbenders Grow up to 2 feet long and are the world's third largest salamander.

The Nature Center is open 7 days a week, 10 AM-3:30 PM except for Thanksgiving Day, Christmas Eve, Christmas Day, and New Year's Day. Admission is $10.95/adults $9.95/seniors and $6.95 for children thirteen or younger. It is located at 75 Gashes Creek Rd., a ten minute drive from Asheville's Arcade building.

White Squirrels

ASHEVILLE AND WESTERN North Carolina never ceases to amaze me. Just when I think I have written everything there is to write about, something new pops up--like the White Squirrels Festival. That's right, I said white squirrels. Not only are they real, they are celebrated by the people of Brevard, NC.

First, let me tell you about the town. It is a thirty-five-mile drive, or bike ride, from the center of Asheville's downtown area, the Grove Arcade. Brevard is the gateway to endless outdoor adventures, including hiking, waterfall hunting, fly fishing and biking. It is a top destination for cyclists of all types—mountain, and road cycling—with excellent cycling shops where guides and equipment are always available. It has over 300 miles of epic single track in the area's pristine forests. And the small town is full of shops, galleries and wonderful restaurants and eateries.

The town's unique claim to fame is that Brevard is the home of the famous white squirrels. In fact, Brevard is host to one of the most established white squirrel colonies in the country. They have flourished in Brevard since escaping from an overturned carnival truck in 1949. Brevard's squirrels are not albino. Albino squirrels have pink or blue eyes and no pigmentation at all. Brevard's are a color variation of the Eastern gray squirrel. And they are easy prey for predators due to the lack of camouflage afforded by their color. Brevard's squirrels have thrived despite this susceptibility in part because of the density of area trees and the fact that town residents put out feeders to encourage the squirrels. Residents of Brevard have a strong civic pride for their white squirrels. So much so, that the town enacted a protective ordinance in 1986, which makes it unlawful for any person to hunt, kill, trap, or otherwise take or harm their squirrels.

The town celebrates their wonderful little critters by hosting the yearly White Squirrel Festival. The festival has been described as a nutty, family fun party over the Memorial Day Weekend. Music is a major part of the event with 14 free concerts featuring national and international performers. And there is always plenty of food, art, and crafts. The Southeast Tourism Society named the White Squirrel celebrations as one of the Top 20 May festivals. A word of warning--dogs are not allowed during the White Squirrel Festival for obvious reasons.

From Downtown Asheville, take I-26 East to Exit 40 and follow Highway 280 to Brevard.

When the town is not celebrating its famous wildlife creature, they find something else to party about. Every month there is something going on in Brevard. Check out the website, https://explorebrevard.com/. The town is a vibrant live music community and home of the world-renowned Brevard Music Center, the Summer Music Festival, and the Porter Center for Performing Arts. There is always plenty of music for partying in Brevard.

Wine Country

ASHEVILLE HAS LONG been called Beer City, but what you may not know is that the Travel Channel named Asheville in the top ten cities for wine snobs. North Carolina is home to more than 100 wineries with 20 in the mountains around Asheville. The Biltmore Estate in the heart of the city is the most visited winery in the country and is open 365 days a year. Another, Burntshirt Vineyards, features a 10,440-square foot winery with a 1,700-square foot barrel room equal to the best of European chateaus. It is only about a thirty minute drive from Asheville, and it is open Sunday-Thursday, 12-6 PM & Friday-Saturday 12-7 PM, with tours at 2 PM every day. And if you want to make a day of it, there are two nearby clusters of multiple wineries, the Tryon Foothills wineries, and Hendersonville Wine Country. The Tryon Foothills has five wineries and it's an easy 45 mile drive from Asheville. Hendersonville has three along a ten mile scenic drive through apple country.

Tryon wineries include:

- Parker-Binns has six wines for tasting and on Sunday, winemaker and owner, Karen Binns, will dish up complimentary brick oven pizza.

- At Overmountain Vineyards, you need to book in advance for their $35.00 per person special tasting, and weather permitting, you can enjoy your wine from their outdoor areas overlooking the vineyard.

- The Russian Chapel Hills Winery produces several varietals including Cabernet Sauvignon, Merlot, Chardonnay, Sauvignon Blanc, and a wonderful dessert wine.

- Mountain Brook Vineyard is a small boutique family winery producing Pinot Grigio, Rose, as well as Chardonnay and Cabernet Sauvignon. Currently, they are only open Wednesday and Monday afternoons.

- Green Creek Winery is another small winery. You can enjoy the day's end on their patio sampling a few wines or their wine-flavored foods that include ice cream and chocolates. They are open Thursday-Sunday from one to five.

Hendersonville Wine Country's three wineries include: South Creek Winery, a boutique winery farm that offers tastings in its Italian Renaissance Farmhouse. Their wines include Cabernet Sauvignon, Merlot, Cabernet Franc as well as blends. They are just off I-40 at exit 90—2240 S Creek Rd.; Silver Fork Winery (six miles from South Creek), that produces Bordeaux style reds as well as Chardonnay, Rose, Cabernet Franc, Cabernet Sauvignon and Merlot; and Lake James Cellars, a family winery located near the beautiful lake of the same name. Lake James's tasting room is a restored textile mill where you can sample wines handcrafted from local fruits—dry reds and whites as well as fruity and sweet wines. These wineries are usually open Wednesday through Saturday, from 11 to 5 and on Sunday from 1 to 5. But it is a good idea to check ahead of time.

A final word of advice, when visiting multiple wineries in the same day, book a car service or have a designated driver! Those numerous small sips of wine can quickly accumulate in too much wine to be driving. Asheville has several car services that can be booked for day trips and wine tours. Two of those include Asheville Premier Transportation at (828) 407-0221 and Backcountry Butler at (828) 808-4416.

EXPLORING ASHEVILLE
PART THREE

∞

Paranormal Events, Mysteries, and Ghost Stories

Introduction

IF ASHEVILLE WERE a person, we would say it suffers from DID, Dissociative Identity Disorder or multiple personalities. But as a city, it celebrates that cultural diversity. Walk its streets and the person next to you is just as likely to be a billionaire as a hippie, and if not, then they are likely to be an artist, a professed witch, agriculturist, author, sculptor, tagger or grafitero, botanist, genius, social drop out, farmer, shepherd, cattleman, creamer, brewer, vintner or just a poor olde mountain boy or girl. It is that diversity, Asheville's many faces, that has given it its unique culture.

But at Asheville's roots are the faces of mountain people— descendants from generations of settlers, immigrants, native Americans and slaves with a tradition of witches, ghost, myths, and folklore. That penchant for the paranormal has now been reinforced by modern day psychics and seers—drawn to the city and its surrounds by their belief that its quartz landed mountains emit energy and power beyond the understanding of humans. They say that energy causes things in the mountains to die slowly—their spirits linger.

Asheville cultural diversity it why it is called many things—Weirdest, Happiest, Quirkiest, Most Haunted Place in America, Santa Fe of the East, New Age Capital of the World, Paris of the South, Sky City, Beer City USA, and Land of the Sky. It is also said to have many secrets, mysteries, and legends—some factual, some alleged, some exaggerated and some hard to believe at all.

Part three tells the stories of those secrets, mysteries and legends including alleged paranormal events and ghost stories.

Chicken Alley

ONE OF THE most haunted streets in Asheville is less than a mile from the Arcade Building. It is just off Woodfin Street. It is actually an alley, Chicken Alley, a narrow walkway between North Lexington Avenue and Carolina Lane. As you approach the alley, you will pass by Building #6 on Woodfin Street with its tiny mouse doors. But the landmark that will announce your arrival will be the giant Chicken Mural painted by Asheville artist, Molly Must. While the mural celebrates the area's rich agricultural heritage, it is the ghost of Dr. Jamie Smith that attracts many of the alley's visitors.

In the late 1800s, Ashville had a rough and raunchy side. Asheville's nearby forest and the navigable French Broad River fostered a growing logging industry in the area, and Asheville was where loggers went for entertainment and "good times." And the Broadway Tavern at Chicken Alley was one of their favorite spots. Asheville's Dr. Jamie Smith was one of its prominent physicians, although on the side he is said to have counted many of the loggers among his clients for treatment of injuries and social disorders. He too enjoyed the "good times" and was a regular at the tavern. Dr. Smith stood out from the other men in route to and from the tavern for his unusual attire—a wide-brimmed black fedora hat and long duster style coat with a silver topped cane in one hand and a medicine bag in the other. On his last visit to Chicken Alley's Broadway Tavern, Doctor Smith met his end. He arrived just as a bar brawl raged and while trying to stop the fighting, he was stabbed in the heart and died instantly. A year later in 1903, the tavern was destroyed by fire.

People say that things die slowly in the quartz laden mountains—especially those who meet a tragic or untimely end. So it seems with Dr. Jamie Smith—his spirit lingers. Late at night (since his death in 1902—now well over 100 years) those who live in Chicken Alley and people passing through it have reported hearing a cane tapping on the pavement or seeing a man lurking in the alley—a man in a long coat and wide brimmed fedora and a silver topped cane.

[Author's Note: Some say Doctor Smith's spirit is looking for revenge, but most locals say he just wants another drink before departing his earthly bonds. As for the mouse doors, they are the subject of another story, TINY DOORS, in just a few more pages.]

More about the Chicken Alley Mural from https://www.muraltrail.com/asheville-murals.htm:

Completed in 2011, Asheville NC. 200 square foot mural with a 10-ft. rooster welcomes you to Chicken Alley. Designed and painted by Molly Must. The design of this mural interprets the history of the chicken-processing plant owned by Sam and Argie Young of Asheville, for which the alley is named. Sam and Argie's granddaughter, Sandra Gudger (the only remaining family member with memories of the business), contributed stories and photographs to the project. Sandra's memories are a testament to the rich agricultural heritage of not just her bee-keeping, poultry-raising family, but also of South Lexington Avenue, where an Asheville farmers market and many farm-supply shops used to be. Sandra is depicted in the mural as a young woman holding a jar of honey out to her viewer, with her pet black snake named "boy" at her feet. Molly collaborated with Sandra in writing a poem further illustrating her visual memories, which is painted on the chicken alley mural.

Church Ghosts

As a visitor to Asheville, the Basilica of St. Lawrence will be on your list of sites to visit because the guidebooks will tell you it is an architectural wonder. It contains no supporting beams. The entire structure including the center dome is built using only masonry materials—bricks, stones, and tiles. Its dome is reputed to be the largest freestanding elliptical dome in North America.

What the guidebooks may not tell you is that you may encounter the ghost of its architect, Rafael Guastavino, wandering its halls or encounter the spirits of his wife and child as they search for husband and father. You see, the architect and master builder of this masonry monument is buried within the walls of the Basilica.

When you enter the Chapel of Our Lady within the Basilica, the focal point is a white marble sculpture of the Virgin Mary being assumed into Heaven. If you turn your back to this statue, you will see a blue tiled door with a cross in the center. That door is the entrance to the tomb of our ghost, and it is never locked! Inside the decorative door is a massive cement-lined door, the entrance to the crypt of Rafael Guastavino.

Why is the spirit of Guastavino so restless that he roams through the church seemingly searching for something? The story is that on this deathbed in 1908, he voiced three wishes to his son. The first was that his son finish the church still under construction. The second was that he be buried in the church which he considered to be the pinnacle of his work as an architect. And the third, which has gone unfulfilled, was that his wife and child be interred in his tomb upon their deaths.

Why was that third dying wish denied to the church's master builder? The blame seems to point to city officials, who sometime after his death banned the burial of bodies on any land, public or private, other than designated cemeteries. However, that may have just been all that was needed for the Catholic Church officials who had apparently turned a blind eye to Canon Law 12422 in the case of Guastavino. That Law provided that "bodies are not to be buried in churches unless it is a question of burying in their own church the Roman Pontiff, cardinals, or diocesan bishops, including retired ones." Local Church leaders had bent the rules when it came to the builder of their grand new Basilica, but after the City's action they were not willing to do so for the rest of the family. Guastavino's wife, Francesca, and his daughter, Genevieve, rather than resting at his side, are buried in the nearby Riverside Cemetery. There are reports that their sprits wander beyond the gates of Riverside to stalk the corridors of the Basilica searching for the husband and father whose tomb they were to have shared.

In addition to unexplained sightings of images that appear and disappear as quickly, church members and staff report unusual cold patches, flickering lights, and doors that open and shut for no particular reason.

Brown Mountain Mystery

IF YOU ARE up for a late night adventure, Asheville is only a little over an hour drive from one of the great unsolved mysteries of the mountains—the Brown Mountain Lights. The lights are a phenomenon in the Pisgah National Forest—ghostly orbs that rise out of the land floating over Brown Mountain and the Linville Gorge area. Sometimes they move randomly over the vista and at other times they move as if intelligent—following and avoiding.

The phenomenon has been investigated countless times, and they are continually studied and photographed by students at Appalachian University without finding an explanation. Nor are the lights a recent discovery. The Cherokee and Catawba Indians had their legends for explaining the lights. Native American tribes battled over the land. One of their legends holds that the souls of Indian maidens are searching with torches for their warrior lovers who never returned from battle. Civil War soldiers wrote home about their frightening experiences with the lights—tales of lights that seem to follow them through the woods. The early mountain settlers had their own ghostly explanations—lantern-carrying spirits searching for the master of the house who never came home from his last hunting trip. The notoriety of the lights inspired the movie *Alien Abduction*, and the lights were also featured in an episode of *X-Files* in 1999.

If seeing these mysterious lights is on your bucket list, the easiest way to secure a front row seat is to drive 70 miles to Brown

Mountain Overlook on a moonless night. Unfortunately, although the overlook will give you that front row seat, it will not guarantee success. The lights appear only sporadically. While they do so throughout the year, October and November seem to be the months they are seen most consistently. Locals say the best chance of experiencing the phenomenon is after a rainfall. For the adventurous, there is another way to view the lights. Wiseman's View is a 55 mile drive from Asheville and involves a short hike to the Wiseman's Overlook. Be sure to take flashlights because the trail is unlighted. In the daytime, the overlook provides a spectacular view of Linville Gorge. But at night the view is transformed into silhouettes. You will be looking over Table Rock and Hawksbill Mountains toward Brown Mountain beyond that ridge. The view is the area of the ghostly lights that have baffled scientists, government researchers and local residents alike and to this day no one knows what natural or unnatural forces are behind them.

Some say the quartz laden mountains have an energy all their own—crystal powered vortexes transferring energy from an unknown source with alleged paranormal connections beyond our understanding.

To reach Wiseman's View take I-40 to Marion. Take exit 81 and turn left on Sugar Hill Road. Go about 3 miles to US 221 North. Drive US 221 for about 24 miles to the community of Linville Falls. Turn right onto NC Highway 183. Go one mile to the large Linville Gorge sign on right turning onto the Kistler Memorial Highway (also known as 1238 and old NC 105). Drive four miles to Wiseman's View. Brown Mountain Overlook is only about 14 miles from the Wiseman's location on Highway 181 between mile marker 20 and 21.

Or, keep it simple by entering "Wiseman's View" in your car's GPS.

Byrish Haus Ghost

THE BYRISH HAUS Restaurant & Pub located at 1341 Patton Ave featuring German dishes is now closed, perhaps a victim of COVID-19 pandemic. Its prospects for the future are unknown. But what is known is that the paranormal activity at the facility attracted considerable attention. It started with objects being tossed about in the kitchen area and barstools being knocked over by some unknown force. Then, there were reports of shadowy forms moving around the building. The owners reached out to Joshua Warren, an author and a worldwide recognized expert in paranormal investigations.

Asheville, no stranger to the paranormal, has been called the most haunted place in the United States. So, Warren had no trouble organizing a séance with a variety of psychics, sensitives, and practiced ghost hunters. Marla Hardee Milling in her book, *Legends, Secrets and Mysteries of Asheville*, reported that as the séance began, things started to change—electromagnetic meters registered activity, a pendulum held by a woman began swinging, another psychic burst into tears experiencing an intense feeling of grief. Some reported feeling touched by something. The temperature in the room suddenly became very cold and a vibration was felt through the table. A Ouija Board spelled the letters O H. Someone in the group suggested O.C. Hamilton as a possibility for the meaning of the letters O H. Subsequent research disclosed that O. C. Hamilton was, in fact, John Joseph Carroll, a Roman Catholic priest who assumed the new name to keep his secret that as a priest he had impregnated a woman lover who he married as Hamilton and moved from Chicago to Asheville.

However, there was another connection. In about 1897, Hamilton built a home that Gus Adler and wife Emma purchased in the late 1930s and converted it into a wine and dine restaurant. Initially, it was called the Old Heidelberg, but Adler changed the name to Sky Club in 1942 due to the growing anti-German sentiment of World War II. Gus died tragically in a 1952 fire caused after he fell asleep in bed with a cigarette. Emma continued running the Sky Club frequented by stars Robert Mitchum, Fess Parker, Susan Hayward, and Grace Kelly when in town filming movies. The theory was put forth that Adler's spirit could be connected with the Byrish Haus haunting. Adler had been close friends with the prior owner of the 1341 Patton Ave property, Gus Kooles. And he frequently visited what was then the Barbeque Inn. There is also the heavy German connection between Adler, Kooles and the opening of this new German restaurant, the Byrish Haus.

Joshua Warren organized a blessing of the place to make peace with the spirits. While Hamilton's spirit may have been among those troubled souls remaining in the restaurant, the owners were convinced that Gus Adler was also one of the spirits involved. They placed a framed announcement on the wall that included Adler's picture and biographical information as well as an explanation that the building was haunted. The Byrish Haus building currently has a sign in the window advertising its "Availability" to anyone interested in reopening the restaurant or acquiring the property. Whoever does may get more than they bargained for!

Ghost Tours

ASHVILLE IS A strange, haunted city. Psychics travel here from all over the globe to explore its mysterious vortex energy and to investigate paranormal activity. So, it should not come as a surprise to learn that ghost tours are a big Asheville attraction.

Haunted Asheville is owned by one of the world's preeminent paranormal investigators, Joshua P. Warren. They are the oldest provider of Asheville ghost tours. You can book tours that promise to send chills down your spine by going to www.hauntedAsheville.com. You have several tours to choose from. The website lists the following:

> Classic Walking Tour—*See Asheville's haunts up close and personal for approximately 2 hours. Our guides will lead you safely through the streets of downtown Asheville, providing storytelling thrills and chills, on this family-friendly experience. It's our business to send you home with great memories of Asheville and stories for a lifetime.*

> The Supernatural Tour—*This two-hour walking tour is the ultimate for adult intellectuals who want to take a step outside the bounds of a usual tourist experience. Your knowledgeable guide will explain what Freemasonry is about and explore the conspiracies with you. We will pass through some alleyways where dark and tragic events have transpired. You'll then get the full scoop on*

our local vampires, witches, and ghouls. You learn about tribal rites in Pritchard Park, dark spirits on Church Street, Native American mysticism, and much more.

Biltmore Village Mystery Tour—*Walk with us through beautiful, historic Biltmore Village and learn the dark secrets of this quaint section of Asheville. This sixty to ninetyminute walking tour is full of mystery and wonder, and fun for the whole family. Discover the stories behind, chilling ghosts that wander the old village, the weird Nazi occultist who opened a portal there, the kangaroo that appeared from another dimension, an insane asylum that will make your blood run cold, Asheville's secret serial killer the Enigmas of All Souls Cathedral and, the curse of Vanderbilt's lawyer, Samuel Reed.*

Asheville's Blue Ridge Mountains are the oldest in the country, and hold the remnants of Native American spiritualism, the bloody Civil War, and some of history's most dynamic personalities—Vanderbilt, Pack, Reynolds, Coxe, Lipinsky, O. Henry, Wolfe, Guastavino and Grove, among others. Visitors to this unique place where things are said to die slowly should never leave without having discovered the paranormal Asheville with its powerful spiritual and crystalline energy vortex.

Great Book Heist

THE GRAND LADY on the Hill, the Biltmore Estate, has had her share of mysteries played out in its grand rooms and behind its secret doors and passageways. In fact, it was during the filming of the movie *The Private Eyes* that the Estate manager discovered they had become the victim of Asheville's Great Book Heist!

Out of all 250 rooms in the Biltmore, George Vanderbilt's library, an inviting two-story room filled floor to ceiling with his books, often ranks as the guest's favorite. Vanderbilt's book collection consists of approximately 24,000 volumes. The library room contains 10,000 of those books. The remaining volumes are in the den, smoking room, hallways, and in storage at the Biltmore. The strengths of the Vanderbilt collection are 19th century English and American fiction, including many first editions, art and architecture, history, travel, philosophy, and religion.

While Tim Conway, who was starring in the movie, was touring the remarkable library, a Biltmore employee offered to show him a 1756 edition of Samuel Johnson's *A Dictionary of the English Language*, but it was not in its usual spot. Estate managers immediately contacted the authorities when they discovered that the two-volume set, valued at $7,500, was missing. When they hastily inventoried the Estate's collection, they discovered that the apparent book heist was much bigger than just the Samuel Johnson work. The inventory disclosed 234 missing items, including an $80,000 portfolio of Goya etchings, a 1797 copy of *The Book of Common Prayer*, Edmund Spenser's *The Fairie Queen*, Muybridge's 1887 *Animal Locomotion* worth $100,000, volumes by Oscar Wilde, Lewis Carroll, the Brothers Grimm, and other items.

Local authorities called in the FBI, and agents said they believed the case to be "one of the largest of its kind in the United States."

The mastermind for the theft was an unlikely thief, but one not very adept at the clandestine profession he had chosen. Unlikely because he was a well-educated Harvard graduate. During 1979 and 1980, he had worked as a nighttime guard at the mansion. He was Robert Livingston Matters but also used the alias, Rustem Levni Turkseven. He had another job—one that would make him a prime suspect when the theft was discovered. He owned the Plane Tree Book Store, an antique bookbinding shop, located in downtown Asheville. Once the FBI focused on Matters, the pieces began falling in place. It seems Matters had been suspected of antique book thefts from other libraries, all reluctant to disclose their loss lest they would be criticized for weak security. The Harvard graduate ultimately pleaded guilty to four counts of interstate transportation of books, photographic plates and etchings and received a sentence of five years in prison.

With the help of the FBI and Antiquarian Booksellers Association of Austin all 234 items were eventually tracked down and recovered from locations across the country and Europe.

Helen's Bridge

THE ZEALANDIA BRIDGE located at 201 Beaucatcher Road is a mere 2 miles from the center of town. It was constructed in 1909 of quarried stone to provide access to the nearby Zealandia Mansion—in its time a massive castle like home. While the bridge was once considered beautiful for its architecture and surrounding scenery, it was the writings of the great author, Thomas Wolfe, who at first secured its connection to the hearts of Ashevillians. In his book, Look Homeward Angel, he described his character's walk with his girlfriend up the crest of Beaucatcher Mountain. Speaking of the bridge, he wrote "…. As they went under the shadow of the bridge, Eugene lifted his head and shouted. His voice bounded against the arch like a stone." Thus, creating a romantic tradition—walking with your beloved under the great arched bridge and shouting up to listen to the lover's echo.

Times changed and events have replaced romance with fright and fear. People now write of the bridge:

> *To sit under that dark bridge is something you will never forget. Cars parked under the bridge always died, the wind always picks up and crazy sounds whip all around the car like scratches or maybe branches of trees scraping only there were no branches."* [Kristen].

> *…will never go back."* [Jen].

...the wind picked up, sticks began to break, and a woman walked out of the woods in all white. [Nick].

...on the roof of my dark gray car was a skeletal handprint [Barbara].

...we both hear a scream (and saw) glowing eyes [Brit].

Those are some of the real life experiences of people brave enough to visit Zealandia's Bridge, now known to locals as Helen's Bridge. The bridge has taken on a dark persona—a haunted place rooted in legend and unexplainable occurrences.

Felicia Huffman writing in *Urban Legend*, retold Helen's story as told by her parents:

Helen was a dedicated mother and lived across from Zealandia on the other side of the bridge. Her daughter often played with the children who lived in Zealandia, so it was natural for her to be gone most of the day. On one unfortunate day, Helen's daughter, who has always remained unnamed, was playing in Zealandia when the mansion caught fire. Being that the construction of Zealandia rendered it virtually fire-proof, the fire only destroyed one room. As fate would have it, Helen's daughter was caught in the room that was engulfed by flames. When Helen went to retrieve her daughter, she learned of her daughter's fate. Distraught Helen raced back across the bridge but stopped when she saw a rope on the bridge. Full of misery and woe, Helen hung herself. The next morning, a construction crew working in the area at that time found Helen's lifeless body hanging from the bridge. From that day on, Helen continues to search for her daughter. Those who have seen her never return to Beaucatcher Mountain, especially after dark. Others have permanent white handprints in the paint of their car, and one man's car never ran again.

Those with the "gift" will tell you that things die slowly in Asheville's quartz laden mountains—so it is with Helen and perhaps her daughter and maybe others—dead souls whose spirits are tied to the Zealandia Bridge.

Hope Diamond

I AM SURE you have heard about the Hope Diamond. It is, after all, one of the most famous jewels in the world—one with its own curse that reaches back four centuries. But you may not have heard of its connection to Asheville before this magnificent blue gem found its way to the Smithsonian's Museum of Natural History. As the story goes, it was once the plaything of a little girl, Mamie Reynolds. Mamie was born in 1942 and was the granddaughter of Evalyn Walsh McLean, the last private owner of the Hope Diamond. As an Asheville toddler, Mamie reportedly buried the diamond in her sandbox or attached it to the collar of her grandmother's Great Dane as it ran through the house and grounds. The grandmother had willed the diamond to Mamie; nevertheless, upon Evalyn Walsh's death in 1947, all her jewelry including the Hope Diamond was sold to a New York jeweler to discharge the Estates debts including taxes. In 1958, the jeweler donated the diamond to the Smithsonian. Today, the diamond is estimated to be worth something in the neighborhood of three hundred million dollars ($300,000,000).

Evalyn Walsh McLean was quite wealthy as a young woman. Her father, Thomas Walsh, struck it rich in the Camp Bird Gold Mine in Colorado. Then, in 1908, she married the heir to *The Washington Post* and *The Cincinnati Enquirer* publishing fortune, Edward "Ned" Beale McLean. Ned Mclean, disregarding the unsavory reputation of the gemstone, purchased the Hope Diamond for Evalyn in 1911 from Pierre Cartier of

Cartier Jewelers in New York. Friends of Evalyn, including her mother-in-law concerned about the legends of the stone's curse, pleaded with her to get rid of the gem. Mrs. McLean was concerned enough to have the stone blessed by a priest. After doing so, she seemed to no longer worry about the claims of the stone's powerful curse. Looking back on her life after acquiring the stone, one must wonder if her belief that she was impervious to the curse was misguided considering the misfortunes which beset her. Her first-born child was hit by a car and died at age nine. The son was named Vincent for her brother who was also killed in a car accident at age seventeen. In another tragedy, she found her daughter, Evie McLean Reynolds (Mamie's mother and the wife of North Carolina's U. S. Senator), dead of a drug overdose at twenty-four. The final blow was the explosive end to her marriage. Her husband, charged with adultery, eventually died in a mental institution, his fortune depleted.

As for Mamie Reynolds, she grew up on a north Asheville estate atop Reynolds Mountain surrounded by 250 acres with majestic mountain views. It was a rustic-modern home of hand-hewn logs and native fieldstone. Most of the time her companions were just her governess, Mimi Palmer, Louise the cook, the caretakers (Mr. and Mrs. Frank Bien) and the stable and farm foreman, Oscar Reese. Although she was known in the press as the world's richest little girl, according to the author, Marla Hardee Milling, Mamie Reynolds had no idea that at 18 she would inherit a tremendous fortune. What happened to her? Surprisingly Mamie Reynolds grew up to become the first woman to qualify for the Daytona 500. While her first marriage was short lived, she had two children by her second husband, Joseph E. Gregory. The Gregorys were dubbed the "magic couple" by the press and shared a common love for living on a farm, racing cars, dog shows and basketball. Mamie was the first owner of the American Basketball Association's Kentucky Colonels. She died in 2014 at age 72.

L.E.M.U.R.—Paranormal Research

UNLESS IT WAS your purpose for visiting Asheville, you probably made the trip without realizing that Asheville is the headquarter for L.E.M.U.R. (the League of Energy Materialization and Unexplained Phenomena Research). LEMUR is the home of the foremost paranormal research teams in the United States. And, if it is something you have always wanted, you, too, can become a Certified Paranormal Investigator by completing LEMUR's online training course taught by famed paranormal expert, Joshua P. Warren.

According to their website, the LEMUR team is composed of experts from various technological backgrounds with experience in electromagnetic field detection, electrostatic field monitoring, infrared and ultraviolet photography, ultra and sub-sonic audio recording, Tesla and Wimshurst implementation, videography, as well as 3-D photography and several other advanced techniques for acquiring data. The team uses scientific methods to investigate paranormal phenomena including ghostly activity. Their field of investigations also includes UFO activity, psychic phenomena, cryptozoological matters, and all claims, experiences, or occurrences that are currently considered unexplainable by the mainstream sciences.

LEMUR investigations have been featured on the Discovery Channel, History Channel, Travel Channel, SyFi, *Ghost Adventures* and numerous other TV and radio programs. LEMUR can also be hired by individuals or institutions wishing to investigate their properties.

The organization was engaged to investigate the alleged ghost of Asheville's Grove Park Inn, the Pink Lady in room 545. Their private work also included the investigation of the haunted Old City Jail in Charleston, South Carolina, and the famous Brown Mountain Lights in the Pisgah National Forest near Asheville. Their work on the LIGHTS earned the cover of the scientific journal, *Electric Space Craft*, published by NASA Hall of Fame engineer, Charles Yost.

LEMUR's president is Joshua P. Warren. He has spent over 25 years as a professional paranormal investigator. Warren is the author of over 20 books and the recipient of the Thomas Wolfe Award for Fiction. He owns the Asheville Mystery Museum and Haunted Asheville Ghost Tours. For more information about LEMUR go to their website, www.lemurteam.com. For the Museum and Ghost Tours go to www.hauntedasheville.com.

Reynolds Ghost

"...YOU LEARN TO deal with it." That is what Billy Sanders, caretaker of the Reynolds Mansion, said talking about the two ghosts or spirits that haunt the Mansion. The Reynolds place is in Woodfin, which for all practical purposes is Asheville or the Asheville greater area. Woodfin is an incorporated city but is considered an Asheville neighborhood by the citizens.

The Mansion was built in 1847 so it has had plenty of time to acquire its paranormal residents. One of its most interesting periods for acquiring guests from the hereafter began in 1900 when Nathaniel Reynolds become the owner. Reynolds, who also owned a funeral home in Asheville, was known to embalm "clients" from time to time in the Mansion. Then in 1920, Nathaniel Reynolds rented this house to the first female physician in Asheville, Dr. Elizabeth Smith. She operated Reynolds Mansion as an osteopathic sanitarium.

This historic building and home to generations of Reynolds, is now a bed and breakfast inn. While there may be more, there are said to be at least two identified spirits haunting it—Annie Lee Reynolds, a spinster who suffered from either depression or tuberculosis, and the other a young child, said to be a daughter of one of the Reynolds, who died from typhoid fever.

The Mansion's caretaker explained, "Usually you see Annie Lee on the staircase, or you'll see orbs or hear a child's voice," Sanders says. "I never say anything, but many guests report similar experiences. That's just part of living here — you learn to deal with it."

This is what The Reynolds Mansion has to say about the reports of it being haunted:

So far, we've had guests report noises in the middle of the night, doors unlocking, shadows on the wall, the smell of perfume in the rooms, and one guest actually saw an apparition in his bed- room. He actually wrote a waltz called Anne Lee's Waltz written for Anne Lee Reynolds who is said to still walk the halls of Reynolds Mansion and still reside in her room on the third floor, now called Maggie's room.

We have all here seen and heard things in this beautiful old house that can't be easily explained away. Lights turning on and off by themselves, doors opening and closing with no one around, and footsteps of someone walking around in the upstairs halls.

To this day we're not sure of the identity of all the spirits here at Reynolds Mansion, but we suspect it's some of the Reynolds family keeping a careful watch over the old family home. Generations of Reynolds lived... and died in this house.

Room 545

ROOM 545 OF the Grove Park Inn is the residence of The Pink Lady, Asheville's most beloved ghost.

According to people I've talked to, she is the spirit of a young woman who fell to her death from a balcony on the fifth floor of the Inn in the 1920's. There are various stories about her, but the most likely is that she had come to the Inn for a clandestine evening with her married lover and that she jumped from the balcony when he ended their affair.

Despite the tragedy, she is said to be a kindly spirit who has entertained and, at times, frightened hotel guests for over a hundred years—especially those who have stayed in Room 545. The employees of the Grove Park Inn are said to be so accustomed to her presence that they treat her as just another part of the tradition of the grand old hotel. The spirit usually appears in the form of a pink mist; however, there have been times where she has shown herself as a full-fledged apparition in a pink ball gown.

The Pink Lady seems particularly fond of children. One of the more notable incidences involves a doctor and his family. When family the checked out of the Inn, the doctor requested that Inn's management thank the young lady in the pink ball gown for the attention given to his children. He told the Grove Park staff how much his children enjoyed playing with her during their stay!

If you are brave enough to book Room 545, do not be surprised when lights, air conditioners, and other electrical devices turn on and off by themselves. The Pink Lady also like to re-arrange things in the room—including your things. And she occasionally likes to wake up sleeping guests with a good tickle!

Mysterious Seely's Castle

MYSTERY HAS ALWAYS surrounded Seely's Castle, also called Overlook Castle and Castle in the Sky. It has had to endure rumors of sheltering a pedophilia cult as well as being the center for Satanic rituals and human sacrifices in the mountains of North Carolina. Its mysteries are evidence that rumors will fill gaps left by secrecy and the unusual. And the existence of a mountaintop English fortress castle certainly meets the test of being unusual, unexpected, and generally unexplained.

The idea for the Castle probably emerged from an inventory problem. The owner had a lot of unused stone on his hands in 1914 when construction on the Castle began. That initial owner was Fred Loring Seely, the son-in-law of Edwin Wiley Grove. E.W. Grove was a patent medicine tycoon credited with transforming Asheville into the most popular resort city in the Southeast in the early 20th century. He gifted ten acres on the top of Sunset Mountain, called Overlook Park, to Seely to build a new home for Seely and Grove's daughter. Seely had overseen construction of the Grove Park Inn for his father-in-law. The upscale hotel was built using native granite rock from the surrounding mountains. Seely had insisted that only larger stones be used to minimize mortar joints. With construction complete, Seely was left with massive quantities of unused smaller stones. That probably was the beginning of the idea for the 20,000 square foot Castle which Seely designed himself.

It is described in its 1980 nomination to the National Register of Historic Places, as a reproduction of Forde Abbey,

Dorset, near London, a mid-twelfth century monastery. Some of its interesting features include the following:

- A Tudor mantel in the library which came from an English manor once owned by Queen Victoria.

- In the Great Room, with 32-foot-high ceilings and massive beams made from whole trees, a stone from the Tower of London and a piece of the Blarney stone were set into the fireplace.

- In the bedrooms, the closet doors were wired by Thomas Edison with switches that automatically turned the lights on when the doors were opened.

- The lions on each side of the tunnel entrance are said to have been from the courthouse in Atlanta that Sherman's army burned down during the Civil War.

Overlook Castle served as a summer home for the Seelys, who spent much of their time in the Far East purchasing ingredients for Grove's patent medicine business. When they were staying at the castle, the Seelys were said to have some impressive guests, including Henry Ford, Harvey Firestone, and Thomas Edison. "Seely attended Princeton as an adult becoming friends with Woodrow Wilson, who was then the president of the University". Asheville native and one time owner of the Castle, Jerry Sternberg, (quoted above) wrote: "Seely later became a significant fundraiser for Wilson's presidential campaigns. During his second term in office, Wilson suffered a stroke, and legend has it that the government was secretly being run by his wife. Every day, to fool the public, they would pretend to wheel Wilson out onto a porch at the White House to enjoy the afternoon sun, but this was just a stand-in. Supposedly, Wilson was actually being kept out of sight in the castle's master bedroom." Another persistent rumor according to Sternberg is that "papers related to the Teapot Dome scandal, having to do with oil leases during the Harding administration, were locked in the enormous safe in the counting house in the castle's west wing."

The last known owner of the Castle is the Wells family. The head of the family, Loren W. Wells, made his fortune as the founder of the Bon Worth Company that manufactured stretch polyester pants. He indicated that it was far too expensive to live in the Castle and that they kept it only for Christmas parties. Loren died in 2018. The rumor is that Omni Hotels & Resorts, the current owners of the Grove Park Inn, had planned to purchase the Seely Castle. However, there is no evidence to date that the property has changed hands.

At one point in the Castle's life, when it was poorly maintained, Jerry Sternberg purchased the property for $40,000 and made it his home for several years. He writes of the adventurous time when he got to play "King of the Castle", in the *Mountain Xpress of Asheville*. To share that adventure, go to www.gospeljerry.com. Prior to Sternberg's purchase, the property was used as the campus of the University of North Carolina at Asheville. Unable to find a buyer for the property, Sternberg donated the property to a religious organization, and it was operated as a mission until eventually purchased by the Wells family. All told, there have been five owners of the property since completion of the structure and grounds in 1924. And despite the mysteries surrounding it, none were Satanic worshipers!

Naked Ghost

IT IS NOT very often that you will hear of a naked ghost. Although a lot of skeptics will point out that all ghosts should be completely unclothed. As they put it: "If a ghost isn't barefoot, it means that shoes have souls, too!"

For me, that argument is lost against the stories of hauntings throughout time. The power that can bind one's spirit to the earth after death defies earthly reason. Thus, to the believer, it is perfectly logical, that a ghost may appear in any form or attire that it chooses or that is cursed upon him or her. If you don't believe me, drive to Craven Street Bridge. It is only about a mile and a half from the Arcade Building and if you go in the early evening hours on a hot day of summer and you are likely to see a naked boy running alongside your car only to disappear before he can cross to the end of the bridge.

Most haunting spirits appear to do so because of their tragic or untimely death--or because they died before they could complete something of great importance. It seems that revenge or unfinished business tends to compel one's soul to return to the site of the offending death.

Sometime in the early 1900s on a hot summer day, a group of young boys decided to cool off in the French Broad River. It was before bathing suits, so they stripped down and jumped in the water wearing nothing but their birthday suits. They were playing and laughing, not aware that they were floating further and faster down the river than usual. The problem was that storms upriver had created dangerous undercurrents and the

French Broad was flowing more swiftly. Time passes quickly when you are having fun, and they were surprised by the fading light as the sun began going down. The river had taken them close to the pilings of the Craven Street Bridge and dangerous rapids. And that is when they noticed that one of their group was missing.

They searched and searched for their missing friend. One of the boys ran for help. Neighbors added to the search efforts and boats and lanterns were used to light up the river. They never found him nor his remains. Searchers surmised that the French Broad's powerful undercurrents around the rocks and pilings captured the swimmer—holding him down while the rapids pounded and dragged him to his death. Eventually, they gave up the search. It was not long after the search was called off that people began to report seeing a naked boy running across the bridge. It might have been a prank, except for what happened every time the boy was spotted. People would call out to the runner, but he never seemed to hear. Then, just as the runner got close to the end of the bridge, he would vanish—disappear into thin air! The poor boy could never get across the bridge.

Ghost stories have always been around. Folklore abounds with stories of hauntings and sightings. Most people believe they are made-up tales But, there is something different here. There are too many stories (in a place filled with smart and intelligent people) to discount them as tomfoolery. There must be some reason why Asheville has been labeled the most haunted place on the planet. Could it be that there is something to the theory of *mountain energy?* Is it the thing that is keeping the soul of our naked spirit bound to the place of his death?

Subterranean Asheville

Enormous wealth was drawn to Asheville during a period in the 1800s and very early 1900s when banks were not particularly reliable for safeguarding deposited funds. Wealth had to be invested in tangible things or hidden away, even buried, to be safeguarded. WWII brought more great valuables to Asheville to be hidden—Including property of the US government and our museums. If some of those hidden valuables, including gold and silver currency, were forgotten, and left in their places of safekeeping, where are they? Are they lying in wait somewhere in subterranean Asheville—waiting to be found?

There are a lot of rumors about subterranean Asheville. But for the most part, no one is talking officially. Homeland Security has invoked a cloak of secrecy prohibiting any unauthorized disclosure. Here is what the public knows. We know that tunnels were used to smuggle bootlegged whiskey and moonshine. Pack's Tavern proudly shows off the entrance to one used from their facility during prohibition. At one time there were underground bathrooms in the city and some people have reported those facilities had access to underground passages. There are rumors of tunnels from the city to the Biltmore Estate that conspiracy buffs say were used for immoral or sinister purposes. While records can't be located, locals say that at one time the city initiated efforts to build a subway system and that at least four underground stops were built. There are indications that an extensive system of tunnels connected various locations including the Battery Hotel, the

Grove Park Inn and the residences of E. W. Grove and other wealthy citizens. We know that there is something under the Masonic Lodge and that the organization refuses to allow excavation, and there are written accounts of underground vaults discovered during the demolition of Asheville buildings.

We also know that the U. S. Government commandeered considerable property throughout Asheville at the start of WWII, including the Grove Arcade, the Battery Park Hotel, the Grove Park Inn, parts of Biltmore, numerous medical facilities, and factories. The Government held on to some of those properties, including the Grove Arcade, for years after the war. During those times, Asheville's remoteness led to it being used as a secret safe harbor for sensitive materials and irreplaceable items of great value.

If rumored tunnels existed, what were they used for and what did they hide? And to the extent that they did exist as a connected system of underground passages, that system is now broken because of time, nature, and disruptive construction and demolition projects. What remains is a series of disconnected underground spurs and vaults with their individual access and egress gone, covered up, lost, and forgotten. So, look carefully as you walk the streets and alleys of Asheville. Someday a sink hole is likely to open, and a lucky person may fall or stumble into a buried fortune!

Tapping Ghosts

TAP, TAP TAP—THAT is the sound of Asheville's oldest ghosts. And let this story caution you from walking late at night past the Asheville Botanical Gardens.

In 1800, the population of Asheville was 38 and had grown to only a couple of hundred by 1835. In those early years, it was not always the most civilized of places with plenty of ruffians about. One of the earliest ghost stories told about Asheville involves just such characters. Two accused horse thieves, William Sneed and William Henry were executed in Asheville in the year 1835. A local man named Holcombe accused them of stealing his horse. The two 24-year-old Tennessee men reportedly lived a life of debauchery and sin, making their way across the Southern states on gambling jaunts and eluding the long arm of the law. Thousands of people of all classes traveled miles to see them hanged.

Writing in his weekly column for the *Citizen-Times*, historian Rob Neufeld wrote about the event:

Rev. Thomas Stradley, founder of the Mount Pleasant Baptist Church (later First Baptist Church), was seeing to the prisoners. "I had great pleasure in visiting them whilst in irons," Stradley wrote in a letter published on June 17, 1835, in The Biblical Recorder, a Raleigh newspaper. He was greatly impressed with the young men's character for they "met their tremendous death with the most becoming behavior and fortitude I ever witnessed or heard of." This, despite the fact that they confessed only to intemperance and gambling, the horse they'd allegedly stole from a man named Holcombe actually having been won in a card game.

The reverend was not alone in his misgivings about their guilt. The men claimed that they had won the horse playing cards with Holcombe. And the two young men were said to have been married and had children back in Cocke County, Tennessee. There was even a petition circulated to pardon the condemned, saying, "No son of a woman should suffer the death penalty for the foal of an ass." Despite their claims of innocence, the two were executed on May 29, 1835, near the current location of the Asheville Botanical Gardens.

...Black caps were put over the condemned men's heads, the signal was given, and the double trap doors triggered opened. ...they did not fall clear down, but only part of the way," and the hanged men tried to gain purchase with an awful scrabbling with their feet on the diagonal boards of the partially opened trap door.

To this day there are many people who when walking late at night near the Botanical Gardens claim to hear the tapping, (tap, tap, tap), of the condemned gamblers toes as they were strung up and dangled from the gallows.

Witches Tree

ASHEVILLE HAS ITS own coven of witches! Oldenwilde, a traditional Wiccan Coven, was founded on Samhain (Halloween) in 1994. They describe themselves as a group of witches who use ancient magical principles for the betterment of life, the continuance of the Universe, and the glorification of the gods. They apparently recognize many gods, but the two primary deities are Hecate, the Lady of the Night, and Herne, the Lord of the Hunt and they celebrate their own set of holidays, Halloween being the favorite:

- Samhain (Halloween) on Oct. 31

- Yule (Winter Solstice) around Dec. 21

- Imbolc (Candlemas) on Feb. 2

- Ostara (Spring Equinox) around Mar. 21

- Beltane (May Day) on May 1

- Litha (Summer Solstice) around Jun. 21

- Lughnasadh (Lammas) on Aug. 1

- Mabon (Fall Equinox) around Sep. 21

The Coven states that its members specialize in different magical talents, contributing to rituals, elements such as spells, chants, songs, and dances. But they view as an important role forewarning of the future. To do this they draw from prophecy, divination, astral planes, and past-life regression. They rose to prominence in Asheville over the county's plans to cut down an ancient magnolia tree in front of the Asheville City hall. Witches consider the tree to be a living soul. The magnolia tree now called the Witches Tree was targeted for destruction to clear the way for condominiums.

Lady Passion led a sit-down protest through rain, shine, and even snow and ice to save the tree from death by a developer's chain saw. The land that was home to the Tree was deeded in perpetuity for public use more than a century ago by philanthropist, George Willis Pack. She voiced outrage over the officials' secret sale of public parkland to a developer (Stewart Coleman), who intended to sacrifice the living beings (trees) and erect a concrete condo to shelter rich people. The attention triggered a lawsuit from Pack's heirs contending that the deal breached their ancestor's deed, and it gathered the support of citizens of every faith and background. The protest became rituals with Pagans, Wiccans and others encircling the tree and chanting spells to protect it, and according to Lady Passion chanting, "*Barbarous Words of Power to thwart the developer.*"

Eventually, the Witches Tree won and remains "undaunted" in front of City Hall to this day. The developer abandoned his condo project and instead restored the adjacent historic Hayes and Hopson building which now serves Asheville as Pack's Tavern. The Hayes and Hopson property was built in 1907 by a local lumber supply company and is one of the oldest buildings in Asheville. It was rumored at one time to have been the distribution center for moonshine using the lumber sup-ply front and a little underground tunnel across Eagle Street. Asheville won on several levels thanks to its Witches. The Tree was saved. Another historic building was saved and restored, and Asheville got a great people's tavern named after one of the city's great benefactors, George Willis Pack.

Visiting Ghost

ASHEVILLE'S MONTFORD NEIGHBORHOOD is one of the most haunted places on the planet. Many of old the Montford estates and manors are said to have their own spirits in residence. Even those that don't can have an occasional haunt from a visiting neighborhood spirit. A case in point is the Applewood Manor's visiting ghost. A mere 400 human steps across lawns and fields from the Applewood Manor Bed and Breakfast Inn is the home haunted by the spirit of sixty-one-year-old Mary Cooper, an accomplished pianist. Actually, if Mary had not stopped aging almost a 100 years ago, she would be 156 today. But in 1926, Mary Cooper met an untimely death. Her death was a mystery that competed in the news with Lindbergh's solo transatlantic flight and the mystery remains unsolved to this day. Was she murdered or was it suicide? Whichever it was, it was an unhappy end to her human existence, and she has stayed around just shy of hundred years in the home on Montford Avenue where it all happened. And there is no indication that her spirit has any plans of vacating her home anytime soon.

When Mary pays Applewood Manor a visit, guests report feeling a presence in the parlor, sometimes called the music room. She has never materialized visually as far as we know, but the piano music has been heard late at night when no one is there. At least one guest is alleged to have had a direct encounter with Mary. Of course, we have no way of verifying the account. According to the story, the guest had been unable to sleep and was alone reading a book around midnight when she claimed to have suddenly felt a cold draft in the room. Then there was the sweet smell of a lady's perfume followed by an event that sent the guest flying back to her room. The event that frightened her was a piano key that was repeatedly depressed playing a single note over and over as if a person were standing next the instrument and tapping the key impatiently waiting for our book reader to leave. Applewood Manor's guest doesn't remember which note was being played. Not that it matters, but it would be interesting to know. Maybe Mary was trying to tell folks at the bed and breakfast inn something

So, if you should happen to be staying at Applewood Manor and hear the piano late at night, don't be alarmed. It's just the neighborhood wandering spirit paying the inn another visit. Mary means no harm. She just loves to play her music.

Exploring Asheville
Part Four

∞

Tall Tales from the Rocking Chair Porch

PART FOUR

Introduction

THE SETTING FOR the telling of the stories in this Part Four is the Rocking Chair Porch of the historic Asheville bed and breakfast inn, Applewood Manor (Circa 1912) located at 62 Cumberland Circle, Asheville, NC 28801.

Early on, people coming to Asheville for its heathy mountain climate and for medical treatment usually stayed in boarding houses. As time passed boarding houses were replaced by bed and breakfast inns that became a favorite of tourists visiting Asheville to enjoy the majestic beauty of its mountains, its celebrated festivals, and Asheville's boundless number of other attractions. Applewood Manor is one of those inns. It was originally built as the home for retired Army Captain John Adams Perry and his family.

Perry hired the architect, William Henry Lord, to design the residence in what is now the Montford historic District. The early New England Style Colonial Revival is a 6000 square foot two-story structure of frame construction with a stone masonry foundation, cedar shake siding featuring a pediment entrance supported on Doric columns and flanking porches.

The foundation was laid by the same stonemasons who worked on the Biltmore Estate The floors are pine throughout.

Captain Perry has been characterized as a charming man who found the children in the Montford neighborhood to be entertaining. He was said to have delighted them by making kites and whittling windmills out of red cedar. He probably did so on the grand first floor porch while rocking in his favorite chair where I can image him also sharing stories and tall tales with visitors and men from the neighborhood.

My son, Stephen Collins, purchased Applewood Manor in 2020. On my family visits, I have spent a lot of time on Captain Perry's Porch and in Part Four, I retell the stories told by imaginary friends and acquaintances while rocking on Applewood Manor's Rocking Chair Porch.

Chimney Rock Gold

I WAS IN one of the rocking chairs at Applewood reading a book and a drinking some lemonade when Clyde Hadfield invited himself to join me on the porch. Clyde has a place over near Bat Cave. I understand it's pretty much a tarpaper and hewn log cabin he built himself. Fortunately, there is no lady of the house—he is a seventy-year-old bachelor who ekes out a meager living prospecting for artifacts—pioneer tools left to rot or rust, Civil War things from retreating soldiers and, of course, Indian stuff. He had stopped by the Manor to see if they wanted to buy any of his findings for their little gift shop. I asked him how the souvenir hunting was going. Clyde poured himself a glass of lemonade from the pitcher the kitchen had made for me and settled into another rocker.

"Well, sir," he said. "It ain't going that well anymore. Most of the stuff around Bat Cave and the Chimney Rock Village seems to have been pretty well found already." So, I said, "I guess you will just have to start working another area." "No sir, Mr. Collins, I can't do that." "Why not?" I asked. "Well, it's like this, my artifact hunting is just a sideline. I have really been looking for buried treasure—gold buried somewhere up there around Chimney Rock. Been looking for it for more than forty years. And I'm afraid one of them Asheville tourists climbing that dang rock and hiking up Round Top Mountain will stumble on it before I do." Well, of course, Clyde's explanation that he was looking for treasure sounded farfetched, but I went ahead and asked him how buried gold found its way to such a popular site-seeing spot.

"It's like this, Mr. Collins. A gang of about six Englishmen owned a mine further up north. They were carrying a large load of gold to the coast when they were ambushed by Indians up around Hickory Nut Gap. They kept running and eventually they found a cave. They were outnumbered so they tried to build a stone wall at the mouth of the cave. It didn't save them; the Indians were too strong and killed all of them except for one who hid himself and managed to escape during the night. That Englishman eventually reached the coast. Got himself on a ship and returned to England. According to the story, he was going to organize a party to return to the mountains and recover the gold hidden away inside the cave. Before he could leave England, the man lost his eyesight and had to dictate a map to the gold's hiding place. For whatever reason, the treasure hunters that came back from England were unsuccessful in locating the cave. There was also Collett Leventhorpe who got word about the gold from his family in England. He became a Confederate General in the war, but before that, in 1843, he spent two months using fifty of his slaves to search for it. Like the others, he went away empty handed." The old prospector got quiet, leaned back in his rocking chair and took a sip of his lemonade. Finally, I said, "Look here Clyde, as you know, I'm a writer and I've written and read some real whoppers, but your gold story is a little hard to believe."

Clyde leaned forward and looked squarely at me. "You know, I'm kind of happy you're not sold on my story. Honestly, I don't think I've told another living soul about that hidden treasure. I guess you just asked in a moment of weakness, and it just all came flowing out. I would just as soon you keep this to yourself. I got this feeling that this is going to be my year.

Something tells me, I'm finally going to find that cave. Well, Mr. Collins, I think it is best I head home." We shook hands and Clyde left me. I continued to think about his story and what he said at the end about being happy that I didn't necessarily believe it. So, I got out my iPhone and entered Chimney Rock lost treasure in to Google. There it was bigger than life:

In his 1941 book, Western North Carolina Sketches, Clarence Griffin retells the tale of a lost fortune near Chimney Rock, specifically on Round Top Mountain.

Cow Counting

IT WAS A windy day and a little nippy, but that didn't stop us from chewing the fat on the Applewood Manor Rocking Chair Porch. There were four of us. Me, of course. Then there was John Parker and Robert Edward Hood. If you recall, Bob, that's what everybody calls him, is a retired military man. The fourth man, from Philadelphia, was a first-time guest at Applewood. He was telling us about his visit to the Biltmore Estate. He had not expected to see pigs or cows and sheep, and he was amazed at the technology involved.

I suppose Bob got tired of listening, so he said, "Well, all that talk of livestock raising and technology reminds me of a story I heard. This happened over in Rutherford County— that's about an hour from here near Possum Hollow Farm. Anyway, this farmer was busy herding his livestock when suddenly a brand-new BMW convertible came down the road and stopped alongside the fence where the farmer and his dog stood. The driver, a young man in one of them skinny suits wearing RayBan® sunglasses leaned over and asked the farmer, 'If I tell you exactly how many cows and calves you have in your herd, will you give me a calf?' The farmer looks at the man, who obviously is a millennial, then looks at his peacefully grazing herd and calmly answers, 'Sure, why not?'"

Then, Bob using his military leader style voice continued to recount the encounter between the two men. "That young feller whipped out his notebook computer, connected it to his Apple cell phone, and surfed to a NASA page on the Internet.

There he calls up a GPS satellite to get an exact fix on his location which he then feeds to another NASA satellite that scans the area in an ultra-high-resolution photo. The young man then opens the digital photo in Adobe Photoshop® and exports it to an image processing facility in Hamburg, Germany. In seconds, he gets an email that his image has been processed and the data stored. He then accesses an MS-SQL® database through an ODBC connected Excel® spreadsheet in the Cloud and, after a few minutes, gets a response. He prints out a full-color, 14-page report on his hi-tech, miniaturized HP LaserJet® printer, turns to the farmer and says "You have exactly 686 cows and calves."

"That's amazing," said the farmer. "Least, you got the count right. Well, I guess you can take one of my calves." He watches the young man make his selection and stuff the struggling animal into the trunk of his car.

The guest from Philadelphia said. "Wow—all that technology is mind blowing!" Bob had this big old smile on this face as he said, "You haven't heard the rest of the story yet. I'm going to repeat it just as they said it to each other. The farmer spoke first."

"Hey feller, if I can tell you exactly what your business is and where you live, will you give my animal back. And maybe 20 bucks to boot?" The young man thinks about it for a second and then says, "Okay, why not?"

"You work for the federal government. You live in Washington D.C., and you haven't been out of the city much at all."

"Wow! That's correct," says the millennial, "but how did you guess that?"

"No guessing required." answered the farmer.

"First, you showed up here even though nobody called you."

"Second, you want to get paid for an answer I already knew."

"Third, you answered a question I never even asked."

"Fourth, you used millions of dollars of equipment trying to show me how much smarter you are than me."

"Fifth, you don't know a dang thing about livestock—or about cows, for that matter. This here is a herd of sheep."

"Now that we are done with all this nonsense, give me back my dog you just put in your trunk!"

Christmas Spiders

IT WAS SNOWING and we already had a good six inches on the ground. I was standing on the Rocking Chair Porch watching some of the younger guests building a snowman. I say younger, but you must understand that for someone in their seventies pushing eighty, people in their thirties, or heck, even forties, qualify as young. Dr. Cornelius Burgos, a retired Church of Christ minister, was also on the porch. He and his wife moved to Florida when Dr. Burgos retired, and this year, missing the seasonal changes, they decided to spend winter in the mountains.

It was that time of the year when people are starting to decorate their homes for Christmas. There were Christmas trees for sale on just about every vacant lot in the city. Holiday shopping was getting in high gear. You could feel the excitement as people counted down the days to Christmas. So, it was only natural that the minister and I started talking about Christmas. I asked Dr. Burgos if the commercialism bothered him. "Sometimes," I said, "the real reason for Christmas seems to get lost in the excitement of tree decorating and all the gift giving and getting."

Dr. Cornelius Burgos's face seem to light up at the question and he said, "Not at all, my friend. I consider it wonderful. Trees and particularly evergreens have been a symbol of growth, death, and rebirth throughout the ages. They represent the joy of life God has endowed us with. And Christmas is a celebration of gift giving. After all, Christ was a gift—the greatest gift of all. I'm sure you remember the words— *"For God so loved the world, that He gave His only begotten Son."*

Dr. Burgos continued. "Throughout the ages Christmas has been about giving. To help the children of our Church understand that we give Christmas gifts and decorate our Christmas trees to celebrate the birth of Christ, I tell them the Ukraine story of the Christmas Spiders. Would you like to hear it?"

"Sure," I said.

"Well, there are variations, but the one I was taught in my village goes like this":

Once upon a time, a poor mother lived with her children in a small home. Outside their house was a tall pine tree from which a pinecone dropped and started to grow from the soil. The children had heard stories of people decorating trees to honor Christ on his birthday. So, they tended to it, ensuring that it would continue to grow and be strong until it became tall enough to be a Christmas tree to take inside their home.

On Christmas Eve, the tree was up, and the mother got busy cleaning the house for the most wonderful day of the year—the day of the year on which the Christ child was born. Not a speck of dust was left. Even the spiders had been banished to a corner in the ceiling to avoid the housewife's cleaning. Unfortunately, the family was poor and even though they had their Christmas tree, they had no gifts to go under it. Nor could they afford ornaments to decorate it in celebration of Christ's birthday. The spiders, another of God's beloved creatures, heard the sobs of the children as they went to bed and decided they would not leave the tree bare. So, the spiders created beautiful webs on the Christmas tree as their gift, decorating it with elegant and beautiful silky patterns.

When the children woke up early on Christmas morning and saw their beautiful tree, they were jumping with excitement. God was pleased, and as the rays of the sun shone on the tree his blessing for what the children and spiders had done in his Son's name, turned the webs into glittering silver and gold making the Christmas tree dazzle and sparkle with a magical twinkle. Thus, the blessed family never suffered from want again. And, to this day, gold and silver colored tinsel decorates Christmas trees all over the world, and we exchange gifts to celebrate the birthday of Christ.

Doctor's Advice

TODAY, THE SUBJECT on the Applewood Rocking Chair Porch was about all the palavering and confabulating about politics and people's health. One fellow is in favor of one thing and this other one is against. Politics and one's aches and pains seem to be all people are talking about these days. Doc Thomason spoke up and said, "Reminds me of a patient I had once." That gave the Doctor center stage on the porch. Doc was retired and most of his patients had gone on to their just rewards. So, he didn't see any reason he should not talk about their various medical histories. On this day, the doctor was talking about old man Dawson.

Dawson was one those dirt-poor farmers out around Weaverville, just up the road from Asheville. He kept a few chickens, a hog or two for eating the slops, and usually a cow. Other than corn, the crops he grew were for eating. For money, he had a makeshift moonshine still made from an abandoned cast iron bathtub and parts from an old car and a refrigerator. Of course, there were also lots of worn-out bourbon barrels and jugs for storing and aging. The corn is what he used to make his moonshine.

It struck me, and maybe a couple of other men on the porch, that Doc knew seemed to know an awful lot about Dawson's moonshine still. Then again, the Doc never said he was a teetotaler. Anyway, back to the story. Doc said when Dawson came to see him, he was getting pretty old—but keeping in mind that corn liquor can age a man, he may have still been in his fifties.

It seems Dawson was worried about his hearing. Here is the way Doc Thomason described his dealing with Mr. Dawson.

"When he came to see me, he said, 'Doc, it's getting so I can hardly hear what anyone is saying anymore.' Well, I looked him over good. I looked in his ears and I didn't see anything mechanical that could be causing a hearing problem. I asked him if his hearing problem was continuous or did it come and go. Well, what do you think he said?"

The other men on the porch looked at each other and no one had any suggestions. Doc laughed. "Dawson said, 'Can't hear you. What did you say?' We kind of chuckled at that because we should have known he would have said that. After we had a laugh, Doc continued his story. "I got right up in his ear and I asked him, you been drinking your own moonshine? Dawson answered me by explaining that he usually had at least one bottle a day, but not any more than that, leastwise not on weekdays. So, I yelled in his ear, if you stop drinking, I think your hearing will come back. That should fix your hearing problem."

The doctor explained that Dawson seemed to be satisfied with his prescription. So, he told Dawson come back to see him in one month. The doctor seemed done with his story. He rocked back in his chair and took a long pull on the iced tea he had been holding. After a few minutes, all of us on the porch were getting restless. So, I spoke up. "Doc, what about it? Did he stop drinking? Did that fix his hearing problem? Did he come back to see you like you asked him to?"

"He sure did, and he was deaf as a stone. I had to cup my hands around his ear as I shouted—did you stop drinking that moonshine like I told you? Dawson looked all guilty-like as he explained, 'Yes Sir, I did and for a week or so and got so I could hear real well, every single word and sound.' Then shaking his head from side to side he said, 'But Doc, it was a terrible thing! Sounded like everything was going to Hell in a handbasket— that's when I decided I liked what I was drinking a whole lot better than what I was hearing!'"

Nail Soup

THEY ARE TALKING about snow tonight, but that didn't stop me from putting on my down jacket and picking a sunny spot on the Rocking Chair Porch to read a good book. I hadn't been there more than a few minutes before Raymond Wilcox showed up. He was delivering some goat cheese. Raymond sat for a spell and then got to talking about his lady friend who has a house across the way on Montford Avenue. He got up and said, "I reckon I'll head over to Miss Jane's and make us some Nail Soup."

Well, of course, I couldn't just let that go, could I? "What kind of soup did you say," I asked? Raymond repeated, "Nail Soup—actually, it's Rusty Nail Soup." "Now Raymond", I said. You're pulling my leg. There's no such thing as Nail Soup." "I beg to differ, Mr. Collins. The men in these mountains have been making Nail Soup for generations, and it has kept us well fed. If you would like, I would be happy to tell you how we got started making our famous soup." To that I said, "You will have to do just that, Raymond Wilcox, because until you do, I'm not believing a word of it!"

"It was like this, Mr. Collins. There was this fellow named Jack back in the 1800s, before the war, who lived in a shack on Bearwallow Mountain. It was a day like this, with snow coming, and he was running short of supplies. So, he headed into town. Jack was getting mighty hungry by the time he got near town. He came upon a little log cabin with smoke coming out of its chimney. So, he figured he would go there and ask for lodging and something to eat. It turned out to be the home of an elderly widow, Mae Thomas. When Jack asked her for lodging, she agreed if he would give her one of his hats. Jack was wearing two hats to keep is head warm. He agreed and gave her the one he had made from a racoon skin. But when he asked for food, she told him her place was no tavern and besides, she didn't have any food in the house.

Jack was a smart mountain boy, and after he had thought on it, Jack said, "Well that won't do. I'm going to make you a big pot of soup to fill your belly and mine." He reached in his pocket and pulled out an old rusty nail. looked at it thoughtfully, smiled and told the widow, "I am going to make you my famous Rusty Nail Soup." To which, she said, "I never heard of such foolishness. You can't make soup out of an old rusty nail."

"But Jack didn't pull back none. No sir, he didn't!" He said, "Why ma'am, I tell you I make the best Rusty Nail Soup in these parts. You just get me a big pot of water on that stove of yours, and I promise to make you the best soup you ever ate." Well, she just had to see this. She got the pot up on the stove and once the water was boiling good, Jack dropped that rusty nail into the pot and stirred in a little salt. In a little while, he began tasting. He would dip a big spoon in, sip and smack his lips. Widow Thomas followed his every move with big wide opened eyes. Then Jack said, "It's getting there. It's a shame though that we don't have a couple of potatoes because that would really smooth it out, but seeing as you don't have any, we will just have to have it plain."

The widow jumped up and declared, "I just might have one or two that ain't gone to seed yet. She began looking about in an old wooden food trunk and came out with two good size potatoes that Jack cut up and dropped in the pot. Directly, he tasted again—smacking those lips. "Now, that's better," he said. "It's a shame we don't have some vegetables to toss in just to give it a little color." Mae Thomas hurried over to the food box and came back with a bunch of wild greens, onions, and carrots. "Oh, that will be fine," said Jack, as he chopped them up and put them in the pot.

He went back to stirring and tasting and smacking. Finally, he said, "The soup is almost ready for us to eat but what would really set this off would be a little meat, but since you don't have any, we will just have to make do." The widow said, "Hold on. I just might have a little squirrel meat and a pig knuckle or two." She waddled off to the food trunk and came back with a good bid of squirrel and four or five knuckles. Jack thew the knuckles in whole and cut up the squirrel and added it to the pot.

After a while he announced with pride. "Get yourself a bowl, it's ready to eat. But you know, what would really be nice is a little bread to sop in the soup." The smell of soup was making Mae mighty hungry as she said, "I just might have a bit of cornbread leftover and she did. Jack filled their bowls and they feasted on his famous Rusty Nail Soup.

And Mr. Collins, that widow never could stop telling everyone about the amazing visitor who made his delicious soup with nothing but a rusty nail!"

Old Blue

NOW HERE IS a story some people have trouble believing, but there are a lot of folks around here who swear its true. It's about the death of a mule, Old Blue. I heard the story from one of the locals while I was whittling on Applewood Manor's Rocking Chair Porch. Years back before there were small tractors for city farmers and SUVs for hauling, a lot of people around Asheville kept a mule or two. Now, Asheville's mules were famous for their unusual stubbornness. Some say they believe their stubbornness was due to the high quartz content of the mountains. People said that the energy vortex affected mules' brains and made the animals think they were smarter than humans.

Well, Old Blue was even more stubborn than all the other stubborn mules around. He saw things his way. For example, if he thought the ground was too wet for plowing, no amount of prodding would make him plow an inch, even if the ground was as dry as the desert. If he decided it was eating time, you fed him, or he would kick on the Manor door until you did— even if he had already been fed. If he decided it was a plowing day, you plowed. If he decided it wasn't, then you didn't! That is just the way it was. So, after a while people just gave up and went with the flow. They did whatever of Old Blue decided was right to do, even if it wasn't.

A number of years back, Asheville experienced a strange year—particularly weather-wise. It seldom gets really hot in Asheville, but that year it did. We are talking really hot—way over a hundred degrees. In the middle of July, on the hottest day of that hot year, Old Blue had decided it was time to harvest the corn. So hot or not, the folks put on their overalls, got some burlap bags, and headed out to the corn patch. They had no more than gotten there when things started popping—pop, pop, pop! It had gotten so hot that the corn was popping. Before long, you couldn't see three feet ahead for the white flecks of corn popping and falling back to the ground.

Then Old Blue started shaking and shivering all over. The folks thought the popping sound had just scared him. But no amount of pulling or pushing got the stubborn mule to move. He stood there shaking and shivering. He would not go back to the barn. Finally, he curled up and laid down in all that popping corn. The humans were suffering in that awful heat, so they just gave up and left Old Blue lying there, after they had covered him up with their burlap bags. They figured he would come back to the barn when he decided it was time to eat.

But he never came back. So, the next morning they went back to the corn patch to fetch him. They found Old Blue on the ground covered up with white popcorn. He was hard as rock and cold to the touch. That darn mule was so stubborn that he had frozen himself to death thinking that he was in a snowstorm!

One Way Cyclist

WE WERE ON the Rocking Chair Porch watching a young fellow ride by on his bicycle. What was strange is that he road by every day at about the same time. But we never saw him ride past the porch coming from the other way. So, like the three old guys we were, with nothing better to do, we started to speculate on what he was up to. Howard Chartwell declared. "It's strange. It's like he is going someplace, but we never see him returning. Something weird is going on here, I tell you! You tell me, how does he get back to wherever he comes from, if we never see him ride back this way?" Well, of course, Howard's declaration was all it took to get people putting evil purposes to things. Jimmy Lee Wilson speculated one thing and Howard Chartwell speculated another. Then Jimmy Lee would have another idea, and then Howard would chime in with another and so-forth and so-on. They covered all the possibilities—he was selling drugs, having an illicit affair, casing the neighborhood for a gang of thieves, etc. Jimmy Lee even went so far as to suggest that he might be an alien —with a spaceship somewhere!

That was just a bridge too far. So, finally I said, "You fellers are just overthinking this thing. Usually, the simplest answer is the right answer. This is probably just his daily exercise routine, or he is riding to work. All your speculation reminds me of the story about a different cyclist that once a week rode across the border to Mexico from San Diego. On his weekly trips, he rode across carrying two saddlebags. The border patrol guards would ask him what was in the bags. 'Sand,' he would answer. 'Open them up,' they would reply. And every time, all the border guards found was sand just as the biker had said. Finding nothing, the guards returned the saddlebags, and the cyclist would continue across the border. This went on week after week. It got to the point that just one guard was assigned to the cyclist.

This continued for six years. Finally, the day came when the guard who searched him every week was retiring. The guard said to the biker, 'This is my last day. I know you are smuggling something across the border, and it is driving me insane. Please tell me! I promise not to tell anyone.' The fellow on the bicycle got this sly grin on his face as he said, 'It was right in front of your eyes. It was so simple you just couldn't see it.' The guard cocked his head like he was thinking. Then, after six years, it finally hit him, and he shouted, 'Bicycles—it was bicycles, right? You've been smuggling bicycles!'

The cyclist, just smiled—then grinned, winked, and continued across the border."

Jimmy lee and Howard didn't say anything right away. But eventually Jimmy Lee spoke up. "Well, if you're so smart, explain to me why we never see our cyclist ride past our porch from the opposite direction. You know, if you ride out one way you got to come back from the other direction eventually, don't you?"

"Fellows," I said, "the simple answer is that the route he rides is a circular route. He rides past us, circles around the streets of Asheville and Montford and eventually gets back to where he started from, never having to turn around and backtrack. That's why we only see him ride past going one way."

"Oh," said Howard. We stopped our detective-like speculation and when back to rocking. It appeared Jimmy Lee and Howard were better at rocking than detecting!

Rocking Chair Wish

A COUPLE OF years back, three old boys were rocking on the porch enjoying the sunny day. Two of them were chewing the fat and sharing stories about how things used to be. Eventually things got around to the subject of mortality and led to the question of how each one preferred to meet his maker. Now please understand, I did not hear this firsthand. Someone told someone who told someone. Nevertheless, a lot of people swear it happened and it happened just the way I'm going to tell it.

The first man was Roy L. Cantrell. He answered to Roy or R.L. It didn't matter which. Anyway, Roy owned a hardware store in Knoxville before he retired in the prior year. He was a devoted family man—5 grown children, eighteen grandchildren and four great grandchildren. Roy said, "I want to know when it's going to happen. I want plenty of time to put my affairs in order and say goodbye to all my family and friends."

The next man was Robert Edward Hood. Bob, as he was called by everyone, was a retired military man and he had that kind of manner. Bob declared, "I want to go with my boots on. I want to hunt and fish. I love these mountains. I want to be in the woods, walking a trail, hunting wild game, or fly fishing. Just strike me dead Lord, when you're ready but please let me be in my boots doing what I love best."

Now the third man, Bubba Watson, up until now had not participated in the conversations that the other two rockers had been engaged in. Bubba didn't talk much. He believed in what Mark Twain had said—*It's better to be silent and thought a fool than to open your mouth and prove it.* Well, that may not be exactly what Twain said, but it's close. Anyway, back to the story. When Bubba did talk, people usually listened. And what everyone will tell you is that when Bubba said something it usually ended the conversation, or at least shut down the conversation on whatever particular subject was being discussed. Bubba was like the period at the end of a sentence. That was it. That is all there was. There just was nothing else to be said on the subject, period!

Bubba stopped rocking—a clear sign he was about to say something, and this is what he said:

> *Well, I'm happy for you fellers that you have decided such an important subject, but I don't want to know when I am going to go, and I don't want to be sweating and dirty out there on some trail with one of them black bears sneaking up on me. No sir! When I leave this world, I want to go in my sleep, just like my Uncle William—and, not like those other three men in his car, scared out of their wits, screaming, and hollering like a bunch of old women.*

Robert Edward Hood took a long pull on whatever it was he was drinking. Roy just slowly shook his head back and forth. But neither said anymore. They just rocked.

Ruinous Wish

It was a wonderful day, not too hot and not too cold—it was just as perfect as you can get. There were four of us on the Applewood Manor Rocking Chair Porch. Two men from Blue Bell, Pennsylvania. One was named Parker and the other was Kevin. It seems their wives were best friends, and the two couples liked to vacation together. Today, the ladies had gone shopping at the Antique Tobacco Barn, so their husbands were just hanging out. The third person in one of the rocking chairs was Ozey Ledford. Everyone just called him by his last name, Ledford. Most people do not even know his first name. Ledford is a native of Asheville—has an apple farm not too far away and knowns about all there is to know about taking care of apple trees. That is why he was at the Manor today. They hired him to check on their trees and to tell them what needs to be done to keep them healthy. He had done that earlier today and decided to enjoy the rest of the day from the perspective of one of the rocking chairs. Of course, I was the fourth man.

When you put four old guys in rocking chairs, they invariably start speculating about something. Today was no different. Today's speculation was all about wishes—if you could have anything in the world, what would you wish for? Kevin was a good Church of Christ fellow and sure enough he was quick to declare, "WORLD PEACE!" The rest of us poo-pooed that and said he was just showing off. So, he amended his wish to immortality, which we thought was a pretty good wish. Parker had been an executive in some big corporation, so I wasn't surprised when he wished for unlimited wealth.

About that time, Ledford interjected that people needed to be careful what they wished for because things don't always turn out like you expect. "In fact," he said, "your wish could wind up ruining your life."

Parker and Kevin stopped rocking and stared at Ledford who had just spoiled their fun. One of them asked, "How so?"

Ledford leaned back in his rocker, looked up at the ceiling of the porch like he was thinking. "Well,", he said, "let me tell you the story my Aunt Lucy told me about a ruinous wish. Now you probably are not going to want to believe this story, but Aunt Lucy, a good Christian woman, swore on the family bible that it was true. And you fellows need to understand that strange things happen in these mountains. There is so much quartz in them hills that the natural laws you are used to in Pennsylvania just don't apply here."

Parker said, "Get on with it. Kevin and I are open-minded people."

Ledford continued. "Lucy was waitressing in an old family restaurant in Flat Rock until she met her maker a couple of years back. One of her regular customers for breakfast was this fellow named Jack. Jack had come back from Vietnam and got himself an out-of-the-way place up in the mountains not too far from Flat Rock. After a few years, he started coming in her place for breakfast. When he did, there was this chicken that followed him right into the restaurant. Jack would sit in the same booth by the front window and the chicken would hop right up beside him in that booth. That chicken never left Jack's side. If Jack got up to talk to someone else in the restaurant, that chicken would be right beside him."

Kevin said, "I'm surprised the establishment allowed him to bring a chicken into the restaurant. Didn't your aunt do something about it?"

"Well, sir, she did not do a thing. She figured Jack was just a mountain boy, and they were always up to foolery. If it was a trick or joke, she wasn't going to fall for it. So, she just treated a chicken in the booth as if it were perfectly normal. Jack ordered the country breakfast. That is a slice of ham, two eggs sunny side up and grits, with biscuits and coffee, of course. After she had taken Jack's order, Lucy said to him, 'And the chicken, what will she have?' The man acted like her question was perfectly normal and he told her to just to bring a little bowl because he had a few pieces of dried corn in his pocket for the chicken.

"Lucy said things got even stranger. When he finished his breakfast and went to pay, Jack reached in his pocket and pulled out the exact amount of his bill including the customary 10% tip."

"It seems to me that having a chicken with you is strange enough," said Parker.

Apparently, Ledford was just getting warmed up. "Fellows," he said, "that wasn't the end of it. No sir. Jack was having that same country breakfast every day, except Sunday when the restaurant was closed until after church. Jack was regular as clockwork and the chicken was always with him. One morning, there had been a terrible ice and snowstorm during the night. The roads outside of town were impassable. Nothing was moving on those steep winding mountain roads. Nevertheless, Jack and his chicken showed up for breakfast as usual—right on time.

"This time, when Jack went to pay his bill, Lucy just couldn't stand it anymore. Particularly because when Jack reached in his pocket and came out with the exact change, it included the increased price that the manager had made just that morning due to higher pork prices. So, she asked Jack how he came to always had the exact amount of the bill in his pocket. That is when Jack told his story."

Ledford decided it was a good place to stop talking and take a long swig from the water bottle he had with him. When he didn't seem in a hurry to get back to telling us Jack's story, our Pennsylvania guest looked like he was about to burst a seam in anticipation, so I prodded Ledford to get on with it. "Come on, Billy Ledford," I said. "Get on with the story, we don't have all day." Right after I said it, I thought to myself—actually we do.

Ledford put down the water bottle and went back to the story. "Jack said he was out in the woods hunting when he had come across the biggest crystal rock he had ever seen. It was as big as a bolder and clear as a mountain stream except for something dark green in its center. It was too big to haul back to his place, so Jack hit it with his pickaxe and it split right down the middle. According to Lucy, Jack said, that when the rock opened a tiny little man in a green suit and hat jumped out of that hunk of quartz. The little man started dancing a jig and singing apparently because he was so happy to have been freed from that big rock. Finally, he wound down and told Jack that for freeing him he would grant Jack three wishes, but he must make them before the sun set. Since it was already late in the day, Jack didn't have a lot of time for studying on it. He tried to think of what to wish as fast as he could.

"Well, I probably do not have to tell you, but by this time everyone in the old restaurant had giving up eating and were gathered around Jack and his chicken to hear his story. Someone shouted out, 'What did you wish for first, Jack?' Jack, replied, 'For money, of course, but I didn't want to deal with lawyers, accountants and so forth, so I wished that I would always have in my pocket exactly amount of money I needed when I bought anything. Almost everyone agreed that was a really smart wish. But there was one doubting Thomas in the crowd. That fellow said, 'Just hold on a minute. If you are telling the god's truth, why are you still driving that beat up old pickup in the parking place. Why don't you have a fancy new Ford-150?'

"Jack explained that it was because of his second wish. 'I wished that my truck would always get me where I wanted to go no matter the weather or conditions of the roads. That why I do not have one of them new Ford or Dodge trucks. You see anyone else driving down from the mountain? No sir, you do not. But I'm here with my chicken, and it was my old pickup truck that got us here.'

"Well now, that won the restaurant crowd over. Jack had made very good and clever wishes. Several people commented that he was the luckiest person they had ever met, and they started talking about what kind of wishes they would have made. That is when Jack, said, 'Fellows, wishes don't always turn out the way you want. My advice is to be mighty careful what you wish for lest they turn out to be ruinous! That is what happened to me.'

"The crowd couldn't believe what Jack was saying. They wanted to know how— having all the money he needed and having a truck that would get him where he wanted to go—that could have ruined his life.

"Jack said, 'Those were good, but it was my last wish that was ruinous. You see, I made a misstate. I wasn't careful. I had been terribly lonely, and I wanted a good woman who would love me just the way I am and always be at my side.'

"Everyone agreed that was a good wish. How could that have ruined his life they wanted to know?

"Jack tried to explain it to them. He said, 'I was getting cocky, and the sun was about to set. I slipped back into my army days—the way we talked as soldiers. That's when I made my mistake.'

"Everybody was on pins and needles. Someone shouted, 'Spit it out, man. What did you do?'

"Jack broke down and cried in front of everyone as he said, 'I asked for a cute little chick to love me and always be at my side.' "

"Well, if that don't beat all," said Kevin. Parker just muttered something, stood up and said, "Kevin, I think it's time we got some lunch."

I looked over at Ledford who was rocking away with a satisfied grin on his face as he said to the departing men—"Yes sir, one's got to be careful what they wish for."

Postscript:

"I'll tell you this, I do not know for sure if Ozey Ledford really had an Aunt Lucy. But strange things really do happen in these quartz laden mountains. So, who am I to say if Ledford's story was true, half true or just plain Tomfoolery?"

Simpson's Hearing

AFTER A WONDERFUL breakfast and a morning nap, I headed for my favorite rocking chair. It was one of those perfect shirt sleeve days you get in the fall. There was four of us—me, Willie Underwood, Doc Thomason, and someone from New York, who along with his wife, was spending the weekend at Applewood. His wife was off shopping, and he didn't have anything better to do than join us on the Rocking Chair Porch.

Willie was showing us his new six-hundred-dollar hearing aids. He was telling us how much money he saved since the ones his doctor had proposed were over $3,000. After a few minutes of hearing aid discussion, Doc said all the talk reminded him of a patient of his. His name was Gary Simpson and he had what he called a winery on Black Mountain. Gary Simpson, he said, was one of those men who was never in doubt even when he was dead wrong about something. Doc explained that Gary's lumbago was acting up and he wanted something for the pain. Doc prescribed some anti-inflammatory and muscle relaxers. With the lumbago taken care of, Simpson told the doctor that he and his wife seem to be having a communication problem and he wondered if his wife was losing her hearing. Doc went on to explain how he gave him instructions for testing her hearing. Then Doc did what he always does to us. He gets our interest up and then just stops like he is at the end of the story. Doc leaned back in his rocker playing with an unlit cigar in his mouth. Finally, I said, "Come on, Doc, what's the rest of the dang story?"

The Doc said, "Well, about a week later, Simpson was back in my office. I figured he just wanted more muscle relaxers, but I was mighty anxious to find out about the hearing problem. So, I asked him how the testing of his wife's hearing had gone. And this is what he explained to me exactly as he told it:

That's why I'm here, Doc. I found out the problem alright! I did exactly what you told me to do. I was standing in the doorway to the kitchen and Mary Jane was across the room with her back to me standing in front of our stove. So, I called out to her. 'Mary Jane what are we having for dinner?' There was no reaction.

So, I crossed over to the center of the kitchen and I called out to her again. 'Mary Jane, what's for dinner?' Still, there was no reaction. She continued doing whatever she was doing at the old stove.

So, I got up even closer. I was not more than eight feet away and I called out to her. This time I kicked it up a little louder and practically yelled, 'Mary Jane, what's for dinner?'

This time she bolted straight up, snapped around to face me, and put those hands of hers on her hips like she does when she is really irritated at me. And do you know what she said to me, Doc?

She said, "You darn fool. I done told you three times, I'm cooking this chicken for dinner!"

Doc had this big smile on his face as he leaned back in his rocker and said to ceiling, "Yep, old Gary Simpson found out the problem with Mary Jane's hearing alright!"

Siren of the Broad

IT WAS ANOTHER nice day, and I had picked my favorite spot on the Rocking Chair Porch to enjoy an interesting book, *Voices of the Winds: Native American Legends*. About that time, I was joined on the porch by Earl Brighton. Earl was a Professor at the University before retiring. When he saw what I was reading, he said, "You know we have our share of legends around here. This was Indian country. And they would tell you that the French Broad River, the Tselica as they called it, is not all beauty and pleasure. It has its dark side."

I asked, "You mean because of its rapids?"

"No sir, I am talking about something unnatural—the Siren of the Broad. As I said, the Cherokee called the river, 'Tselica'. Over the years there have been many young men who disappeared around the rocks just east of here. The Cherokee knew the reason, but not everyone would believe them. According to legend, there exists in the river at that place the image of an alluring woman, a Siren, in the water of the Broad that draws men to her and to their death. There was this fellow, William Gilmore Simms, who learned from the Cherokee and wrote about many of their beliefs and legends in the eighteen hundreds. He wrote about the Siren in Volume 5, if I remember right, of his book, *Myths and Legends of Our Own Land*. He even wrote a poem about it later, titled the *Siren of Tselica*. Only he used the name from a German legend of a Woman that lured men to their death at sea, 'Lorelei'. We studied his writings at the University and I even recited some passages from Simms's book to my students to pique their interest. I still remember the story as Simms wrote it. Would you like to hear it?"

"Sure, let her rip." Earl cleared his throat and then in his professorial voice started his rendition just like he was in the front of a classroom:

Among the rocks east of Asheville, North Carolina, lives the Lorelei of the French Broad River. This stream—the Tselica of the Indians—contains in its upper reaches many pools where the rapid water whirls and deepens, and where the traveler likes to pause in the heats of afternoon and drink and bathe. Here, from the time when the Cherokees occupied the country, has lived the Siren, and if one who is weary and downcast sits beside the stream or utters a wish to rest in it, he becomes conscious of a soft and exquisite music blending with the plash of the wave.

Looking down in surprise he sees—at first faintly, then with distinctness—the form of a beautiful woman, with hair streaming like moss and dark eyes looking into his, luring him with a power he cannot resist. His breath grows short, his gaze is fixed, mechanically he rises, steps to the brink, and lurches forward into the river. The arms that catch him are slimy and cold as serpents; the face that stares into his is a grinning skull. A loud, chattering laugh rings through the wilderness, and all is still again.

"Well, that is a gripping story," I said." But you don't be-lieve that stuff, do you?"

"Who knows for sure, Mr. Collins? I tell you this, legends like this are not baseless. They are grounded in events. Things happen and people look for an explanation. Even now, if a young man were to go missing, I would suggest they look at the Broad around the rocks east of here. Legends are not to be dismissed out of hand."

Special Circumstance

ONE OF THE favorite sports on the Rocking Chair Porch in the summertime is "man gossiping" or chewing the fat as they call it. That is different from women gossiping. When men gossip it's more storytelling, and it is hard to tell a true story from a tall tale. Whichever it is, you can be pretty sure it gets better every time it is told. In fact, a friend of mine wrote a book about the man gossiping at a small town restaurant that he titled True Stories (and other lies) Told at City Café. I always thought that was a perfect way to describe it—and every town has its City Café, or in this case, my rocking chair porch. I was there on the day Truman Goodwin was telling what he heard at the M.A. Pace General Store in Saluda. Saluda is a small town, population 713 at last count, that straddles Polk and Henderson counties. M.A. Pace is an old-time grocery that has been offering jars of locally pickled and preserved goodies and much more since 1899. It's a local gathering place for farmers and ranchers.

According to Truman, Saluda's only lawyer had been telling about a case he had just lost in front of old Judge Baker at the Hendersonville Courthouse. Truman did not remember the lawyer's name so for the purpose of retelling the story, I am going to just call him Lawyer Smith. Anyway, Lawyer Smith was defending the company that owned the eighteen-wheeler that had crashed into old Farmer Maxwell's new Mahindra tractor that had been pulling a trailer with his prize horse, a hog, and his favorite hunting dog inside.

The eighteen wheeler crushed the trailer, and after the crash, the tractor was not exactly in primo condition either. The farmer was suing for the loss of his horse, hog, dog and the replacement cost of the tractor and the trailer. But he was also asking for a million dollars for physical and emotional injury. It was that personal injury stuff that the trucking company hired the lawyer to defend them from. Truman said the lawyer was sure he had the goods on the farmer. And that he could prove that the farmer was not hurt in the accident, and he was just after the lawyer's client because some highfalutin lawyer told the farmer he could get a lot of money from the rich trucking company.

Truman said this is how the questioning and answering went at the trial:

Lawyer Smith wasn't going to waste any time beating around the bush. So, as soon as the farmer was all sworn in and in the witness box, he walks right up to him and says, "Now Mr. Maxwell, at the scene of the accident, didn't you tell the officers that you had never felt better in your life?"

"Yes Sir, that's exactly what I said to those officers."

The lawyer got this big "I got you grin" on his face and said to the Judge. "I rest my case, Your Honor! I ask that you render your judgment in favor of my client."

Well, the farmer twisted around in that witness chair and yelled, "Now just hold on a minute young fellow. You did not ask me about the special circumstances."

"That is irrelevant," shouted the lawyer.

Old Judge Baker adjusted his glasses and looked down on the farmer. "The lawyer's right, Mr. Maxwell. If you claimed you were not injured during the investigation, I'm not going to let you claim otherwise now. I am afraid I am going to have to find for the trucking company."

By now the farmer was all red-faced and he pleaded with the judge. "Judge let me ask you. Wouldn't you have done the same as me if you had been in that special circumstance?"

The lawyer objected, but the farmer's question had made the Judge curious, so he asked the farmer, "Just what was so special about your circumstance?"

"Well, Your Honor, it was like this. When them officers arrived, one of them went over to check on my horse. The horse had a broken leg, and that policeman shot him stone dead. Then he checked on the hog that was laying on the ground grunting, and he shot that hog, too. Then the other officer went over to my hunting dog, Lady, who was badly hurt. So, they shot that dog, too--dead as a doornail, Your Honor. Then they both come over to where I was setting on the ground, and one of them says to me, 'How about you farmer, are you hurting?' Well, sir, under that special circumstance I said what any intelligent man would have said. No sir, I've never felt better in my life!".

That's when Judge Baker banged his gavel and said, "Under those circumstances, this court rules in the farmer's favor."

Valley of the Cross

I WAS ON the rocking chair porch talking with one of the guests, Robert Joyce, a retired banker from West Haven, Connecticut. We had been discussing some of the stories I had written, when Alex Lander said, "Yes, sir, there is some very weird stuff in these mountains." Alex is an artisan carpenter—one of the men who had been touching up the old house. He was there checking on some of the work done by his crew and had over-heard our conversation. When we stopped talking and looked in his direction, Alex continued.

"You ever heard of Valle Crucis? Well, it is a strange little town about an hour or so from here. The name is Latin for 'Valley of the Cross'. It is where three mountain streams come together to form the shape of a Patriarchal cross.

Mr. Joyce asked, "What kind of cross is that?"

"A Patriarchal cross is a version of the Christian cross. Some people call it the archbishop's cross. It is like the cross you see at church or in a cemetery except instead of just one cross bar, it adds a smaller one placed above the regular cross bar. Some people say that second bar represents the resurrection."

That's when I asked Alex what makes this town named after a Christian symbol so strange?

"There is something about it, Mr. Collins---it has a quiet-ness that just seems to set it apart from the rest of the world. The morning mist lingers longer in Valle Crucis than elsewhere in the mountains. But it is at night when the strangeness is strongest—supernatural even. There is an old stone church along Highway 194 just on the edge of town where they say something that could not possibly be from this world has been seen stepping in and out of the shadows of tombs in the church cemetery.

"Now, I am not going to say it's true, but I can tell you a story a guy I know told me. His name is Sonny, and he lives up around Blowing Rock. I have never known him to lie. As he tells it, about ten years ago, he and an army buddy were out fooling around in his truck late one night. They got to talking about ghosts and the army buddy swore he was not afraid of any dead person. Well, sir, Sonny decided to put him to the test. So, he says, 'I got a cemetery that I dare you to walk through. I heard its full of ghosts.'

"For honesty, Mr. Collins, I should tell you that the two fellows were sharing a jug of white lightning, but Sonny swears he was sober as a judge."

I said, "Alex, I've known a few judges and drawing from personal experience, I'm not sure that your friend's comment is all that reassuring."

"Well, I know Sonny," Alex responded. "And he can put away some hard liquor and stay on his feet. Anyway, let me get back to my story. The army buddy was up to the challenge because he didn't believe in spirits. As he said, when your time's up, it's up and that is all there is to it.

"So, Sonny and his buddy headed for Valle Crucis and that old church I told you about. When they crossed the bridge over the main mountain stream, things changed—there was a light fog, and the full moon was so bright that it washed all the colors away. It was like being in a black and white movie. Eventually they came to the church. Its cemetery was bathed in an eerie white glow of moonlight, so the tombs had these long shadows. Just as the boys started to get out of their truck, something made them both stop. Neither one knew what had stopped them at first. They just kind of looked at each other. Then they saw it."

Mr. Joyce was all ears. "What? What did they see?"

"It was dark, and it was big. It came out of the shadows and was running toward the road. The thing jumped the wall around the cemetery landing in the middle of the road facing their truck. Sonny said it was a demon, a snarling devil dog-like thing as big as a horse, with long yellow teeth. And he swears that the demon's eyes were flaming with red fire from Hell! And the smell—it smelled of death and filth that spilled into their truck. Well, the boys were paralyzed with fear. Then it started coming toward their truck. That got Sonny moving! He threw that old truck in reverse and spun it around to hightail it home. Only, the demon kept coming. And the faster they drove, the faster it ran! Sonny said it was gaining on them and both men thought it was going to get them for sure!"

I interrupted. "They must have gotten away, since you're telling their story."

"It seems that just as that devil was about to catch them, they got to the bridge. Whatever the thing was, it stopped right there. It let them go. It stopped at the bridge, on its side of the little river."

Joyce asked, "What made it stop?"

"I've thought about it a lot. Those three mountain streams that form the image of the Patriarchal cross kept that demon from spreading its evil beyond the valley. The demon cannot cross those Holy Waters."

Mr. Joyce seemed to be entranced by Alex's story, but I had my doubts. "Alex, that is a good tale, but are you sure your friend didn't just come across a very irritable black bear?"

"I don't know any black bears with the fire of Hell coming out of their eyes! All I can tell you Mr. Collins is that I am not going to be getting close to that church graveyard at night any time soon—not now, not ever!"

Author's note: I few months after hearing Alex's story I had the opportunity to visit Valle Crucis. The bridge, the three mountain streams, the old church, they were all there exactly as Alex described them, but there were also friendly people, a general store, and a nice winery. It appeared to be a nice quiet little community. Nevertheless, I would never discount Alex's story completely. These mountains are full of strange things— some hard to believe and some that seem beyond this world.

CPSIA information can be obtained
at www.ICGtesting.com
Printed in the USA
LVHW081614271022
731752LV00015B/774